# GAY SPIRITUALITY

EXPERIENCES
IN
SELF-REALIZATION
FOR GAY MEN,
LESBIANS,
AND
ENLIGHTENED
HETEROSEXUALS

## Roger G. Lanphear

**unified** PUBLICATIONS
*Knowledge for the Twenty-First Century*
1050 University Avenue, Suite 103
San Diego, California 92103

**unified** PUBLICATIONS
1050 University Avenue, Suite 103
San Diego, California 92103


ISBN: 0-9625800-0-7

Printed in the United States of America

# ACKNOWLEDGEMENTS

The need for this book is perhaps best illustrated by the requirement to thank my dear friends without using last names. We are still sensitive to some of the ignorance, prejudice, and scorn focused on our community.

I give heartfelt thanks to Ron, Michael, and Drew—three of my very best buddies. In their own ways they helped lay the foundation for this knowledge.

I am grateful to Pleasant for his editing and input. His knowledge of storytelling, his familiarity with these techniques, and his command of the written word made his help and encouragement essential.

To my friends Lightning, Adam, Terry, Dave, Fred, Mark, Valorie, Donna, Bunny, Rick, and Greg, thanks for your enthusiasm and suggestions.

To my Mom and Dad, I love you for your unconditional acceptance of my life and work.

THIS BOOK IS DEDICATED TO
BEAUTIFUL DREW

# TABLE OF CONTENTS

# The Spirexual Experiences

This book is a slice of my autobiography. That was not my original intention. I had no idea I would open my soul to share so many private moments.

For over fifty years I've been a gay man. Like most homosexuals, I lived two lives. In one I practiced law, chaired the local planning commission, and ran for Congress. In the other I slept with my lover, entertained my gay friends, and frolicked in San Francisco.

These two lives never met. Everything I did fell into one or the other. I've published two other books, both from the *establishment* side of my dual personality. They are on meditation, channeling, and tapping the great resources within each of us, without a hint of my sexuality.

This book was intended to be from my gay side as a gift to my gay brothers and lesbian sisters. It was unfathomable that any of my projects would ever cross the impenetrable shield I had erected between my two separate lives. Yet, I believe I may have done just that.

In my non-gay world my sexuality was a carefully guarded secret. Not until recently have I even been open to my parents, and they made the first move. Only with one of my three siblings has my homosexuality been discussed. I have no idea what they think or say behind my back.

This double life came about at an early age. My first lover was a third grade classmate. I often joke I was *ate* before I was nine. That love affair was far more than sex, though. Michael— meaning "likeness to God"—brought me a real taste of the God experience, true to his name. Ever since, I have linked sex, love, God, spirit, and joy into one package.

With Michael, I knew we somehow experienced God when we got to sleep together. At the same time I also knew my parents would not approve. What I did with Michael had to be a secret. No-one told me. I just knew. That barrier lasted nearly a lifetime.

I say *nearly* because it looks like the barrier is crumbling. For the first time, I'm inviting some enlightened heterosexuals to peek into my heretofore very private, very personal other life. To those of you who enter, welcome. Perhaps this small gesture will help destroy the wall of separation.

More importantly, this small gesture may open a flow of love between the gay and the non-gay cultures. We are all one in reality. The barriers we put up are in our minds. They're made of thought, not steel.

Every gay man and lesbian I know wants to be unconditionally loved and accepted by family, friends, and co-workers. No-one likes to be quiet about who they feel they really are. From our side, I know an open communication is welcome.

I've met enough non-gays to know that many welcome us with open arms. Perhaps they are the more enlightened of the heterosexuals. It's a good place for all of us to begin. Tomorrow we can come out to everyone, the foundation having been laid.

There is no more perfect vehicle for us to tear down the invisible barriers than our quest for God, for Self-realization, for peace and love, for enlightenment. The techniques I'm sharing with you just might be such a connector between the homosexual and the heterosexual communities. I like to call these techniques *spirexual experiences.*

*Spirexual* is derived from *spiritual* and *sexual.* Spirit is the common goal of everyone, whether gay, lesbian, or heterosexual. We are all spiritual beings striving to unfold our power and perfection, whether we are aware of it or not. At the same time, we are all sexual beings. All of us have these powerful spiritual and sexual drives in common. Spirexuality is one of our common threads.

My sexual orientation has always been an important part of my spiritual growth. I can't completely share these spirexual experiences— techniques, if you prefer—without presenting them in the context of my life as a gay man.

Nevertheless, all of these spirexual experiences work for everyone. They are meaningful and growth inducing for every gay man, lesbian woman, bisexual, and heterosexual.

The spirexual experiences do bring results. They are both a path to and the reality of enlightenment. A lifetime of metaphysical practice has lead me to carefully select these to share with all who are drawn to this book.

Shortly after my first sexual experience with Michael, I started my search for spirit. My piano teacher loaned me three precious volumes to read by Baird Spaulding: *Lives and Teachings of the Masters of the Far East.* They set my sights high, and I've been climbing ever since.

Many specific spiritual pursuits have laid the foundation for this book. Some include Transcendental Meditation, The TM-Sidhi Program, Rebirthing, Teachings of the Inner Christ, Polarity Therapy, Mahikari, and Reiki. These gave me the tools to tap my inner source of intelligence for the wisdom in these pages.

The techniques I'm going to share may seem too simple to work. Or, my writing style may seem too simple to convey the profound. Don't be fooled. I can assure you from my own experiences that these tools, while very very simple, do work. They will open up a whole new dimension to your life.

I strongly suggest you read this book slowly. Digest each chapter and try its exercises a few days before moving on. Each lesson is a foundation of sorts for what follows.

These spirexual experiences are more than theory. They are a daily, living reality in my life. They have brought me an awareness of who I am, my qualities, and my power. They opened my heart to give and to receive love. They taught me to locate the center of all knowledge we all have and to manifest my true desires. I learned all about relationships, my body, and my soul. Because of these spirexual experiences, my world is beautiful, perfect, and supportive. When I need reliable guidance, I know where to go and how to safely channel my Self and the Masters. I've learned much about AIDS, why I'm here, and how to forgive.

This is what these pages can open up for you, dear reader. It matters not the least that my life as a gay man is the stage setting. The knowledge presented herein is universal. In order for you to benefit, just incorporate these techniques into your daily life.

To my dear gay brothers and lesbian sisters, may these techniques help you to realize your divine worth and your perfect role in the scheme of nature.

To our enlightened heterosexual friends, may this book broaden your appreciation of the personal side of our homosexual lives.

To everyone, may these spirexual experiences bring you an awareness of your God qualities, the peace of giving and receiving love, the joy of manifesting your true desires, a conscious link to your Self and the Masters, a sense of your purpose and perfection, and the development of your power.

To my dual lives and to the dual cultures they represent, may the spiritual awakening of the world crack the wall of separation forever.

CHAPTER TWO

## *The Conscious Connection*

A few summers ago while I wrestled with letting go of a ten year relationship, I helped my friend David run a restaurant on Cape Cod. In many ways it was an idyllic summer. I had an early morning to mid-afternoon shift, so I had plenty of time to ride my bicycle through Provincetown, comb the beaches, take in the tea dance, or people-watch at the town square.

As part inducement to come to the cape, David provided a funky cabin in the woods. I lived alone, but had an extra room for a steady stream of my California guests. The only sign of life around was the adjacent cabin. We were at the end of a long twisting dirt drive. That other cabin was smaller, but three or four fellows crammed themselves in. One was a gorgeous college jock— the kind you sneak a peak by turning out the lights and hope he can't see you staring out the window.

My connection with him was non-existent. An occasional wave when one of us had to wait for the other to drive up the driveway was the extent of it. I assumed he didn't know I am gay.

Late one night the fellows came home very drunk. Loud music and boisterous play woke me up. Then quite unexpectedly, the jock opened his door and screamed at the top of his lungs, "I'll teach you to look at my ass, you faggot." He slammed the door so hard, I could hear one of its panes shatter.

I got up, tip-toed to the kitchen, and peeked through the curtains. I could see him gesturing wildly with two others. Then to my horror he climbed onto a chair and grabbed a rifle hanging on the wall. I watched as he reopened his door, then I ducked down in fright by the refrigerator.

"You fucking queer," he yelled. "My neighbor's a homo! Homo! Homo!"

The door slammed again, and I could literally feel the anger he was throwing at me. My only consolation was that his friends tried to subdue him. I could hear their muffled voices.

"So what if he's gay, it doesn't hurt you."

"Come on now, settle down."

"Forget about him, you're just drunk."

I was alone. It was very dark outside, and for one of the few times in my life, I felt truly frightened. I didn't even feel safe enough to go to my car and drive away. I checked the locks and latched the chains for the first time ever.

To retain my composure, I decided to sit up and center with my Higher Self signal. Centering with my Higher Self is a tool I had been using for many years. It is a simple procedure of going within and consciously locating the core of my own being—my Higher Self, and is one of my favorite experiences. I call it *"The Conscious Connection."* In fact, this is such an important spiritual tool, let me share it with you now before finishing my story. If we gay men, lesbians, and open-minded heterosexuals are to have experiences in Self-realization, we must have solid and concrete awareness of our Higher Selves.

In many ways this first spirexual experience to locate a Higher Self signal is the foundation for all the rest of the knowledge in this book. Take time to practice this technique a few days before moving on. Every day now—for the rest of your life—don't let a day go by without spending time to consciously connect with your Higher Self.

You might be able to get the experience of the Higher Self signal right away, or it might take weeks of daily sittings. It doesn't matter. By just doing this procedure, you'll cultivate your nervous system so eventually the experience becomes second nature. One thing is certain: with time everyone gets a Higher Self signal.

Choose a comfortable place to sit. Make arrangements not to be disturbed: door closed, animals outside, phone on the machine or unplugged. You know what needs to be done. Then close your eyes for a few moments. When you start to feel settled, connect your breath. That means you breath normally, but there is no space between the in and out breaths. The breath is like a huge wheel—just easy, effortless, connected breathing.

Keep your attention on this breathing for five minutes or so. If your mind goes off on a thought, easily come back to the awareness of your breath. Of course, you can have thoughts as well as the awareness of this connected breathing. Just slightly favor the awareness of your breath.

The purpose of this connected breathing is to settle down, to get relaxed. After about five minutes, stop trying to connect your breath and switch your attention to your heart. Notice the feelings in your heart region. Don't try to put feelings there. Just feel whatever is there. It could be waves of bliss, or it could be uncomfortable. If it is not comfortable, know that at some level you're cleaning out some emotional stuff. This relaxation actually speeds up that cleansing process, like a deep sleep helps to heal the flu. With continual practice you'll eventually only notice love or bliss pulsating from this region, but for now notice whatever is there.

This relaxation sets you up to consciously contact your Higher Self and to receive its signal. *Higher Self* is actually a misnomer, because it isn't higher at all. It's simply you in the fullest sense. Perhaps you'd rather call it your soul, or your God-Self, your whole Self, or just Self. The more you practice this experience, the clearer your Higher Self will be and the more comfortable you will be with it.

What you want to develop in this experience is a clear Higher Self signal. That is some indication to you that you are indeed centered— that you have consciously connected to your Higher Self.

So, while you're feeling that love in your heart, notice if there is a pulsation in that heart region that isn't from the heart beat. Silently ask for the signal, then notice if there is some movement of energy you can detect. It can swirl around the heart. It can start at the head and travel down the trunk of the body. It can start in the stomach and travel up and out the head. It can be a simple pulsation in the heart that so resembles a heart beat you may need to check the pulse on your wrist to learn it isn't. This pulsating sensation can take many forms and is your Higher Self signal. Just let your attention remain with it. Thoughts can also be there, but gently keep your awareness also on that signal.

Continue feeling the heart region so that your total sitting time is about twenty minutes. Open your eyes and check your watch or a clock if you want. When the time is up, keep your eyes closed for another few minutes, gradually becoming more aware of your surroundings. Slowly open your eyes, move your body parts easily, and stretch. Not to come out slowly may lead to some roughness or irritability for a short time.

If you don't notice the pulsation after a week of doing this daily twenty minute mediation, then you can ask for a more physical signal. This is some physical movement, sensation, vision, or feeling that you will notice that is involuntary. In that very settled state, ask your Higher Self to give you a physical signal. Be sure to sit so your arms, back, and legs can move. Let your head be balanced, like that little plastic dog in the car rear window. Then innocently wait for something to happen.

When the signal comes, finish your twenty minutes by letting your attention be with the signal. Observe it. Let thoughts roll, but keep some part of your awareness with the signal. Examples of some Higher Self physical signals are: the head rocking back and forth; the head moving from right to left (or left to right); the head nodding; knees shaking; fingers moving; elbows moving in and out; eye lids fluttering; warm areas on the body; sensations on the body; or visions of light, colors, or pictures. The physical signal can literally be anything pleasant that you can notice. However, that's key. It must be pleasant. Focus on whatever signal seems most natural for you, whether a pulsation in the heart region or a more physical experience.

Getting *The Conscious Connection* down pat is the basis of so many of the spirexual experiences you'll learn from this book. It's like the basic recipe for white sauce, if you cook. With that white sauce you can make hundreds of delicious toppings. That's the way it is when you sit with your Higher Self signal. The body of knowledge that opens up to you by just tapping this resource can stagger your imagination.

Some of the tools that spin off from this first spirexual experience we'll go into in this book. When you have mastered all this book has to offer, that's just the beginning. Then you will be open to all the knowledge and experiences in creation. Experience builds upon experience until you fully comprehend all that is. You will be a Master of Creation, and it all begins with this simple experience of locating your Higher Self signal and allowing your attention to be with it.

When I sat down to center with my Higher Self signal while all those gay-bashing insults echoed in the background, I felt genuine fear. As I sat there with the signal, I asked my Higher Self for knowledge that could protect me and calm the situation. The answer did come, as it always does. But wait. Before we get into that, let's pause so you can try out your first spirexual experience—*The Conscious Connection.*

## THE CONSCIOUS CONNECTION
### *Experiencing Your Higher Self Signal*

*Sit comfortably with your eyes closed and allow your attention to be on connected breathing for five minutes, then on your heart region with normal breathing for another fifteen minutes. Notice if there is a pulsation in the heart region that isn't from your heart beat, and focus your attention on that.*

*If you don't notice the pulsation after a week of this daily twenty minute meditation, then ask for another, more physical signal from your Higher Self, such as a movement, sensation, vision, or feeling. When that appears, keep your attention with it to complete the twenty minute meditation.*

*Always end this experience by taking a couple of minutes to slowly open your eyes.*

# CHAPTER THREE

## *Neutralizing Distress*

The jock's door flew open again. I could hear it bounce off the side of the cabin.

"Homo! Homo! I'll teach you to look at my ass." I could hear clicks from the rifle, and he slammed the door shut.

I sat up on the bed, trying as best I could to settle down and get my Higher Self signal—the handle on the peace within. I knew it was there. I had experienced it nearly every other time I unified.

Finally the signal appeared. For me, it alternates between a pulsation in the heart region and a gentle swaying of my head from one side to the other. This time my head swayed, so I focused on that. Then the peace came, like a feeling of love in the heart.

"I'm going to blow your brains out, you faggot," he yelled. His friends laughed in the background.

"Thank God I don't have to buy into his garbage, that irrational fear of homosexuality," I thought. My only concern was his unpredictable violence. I flashed on two friends who had been murdered by homophobes; I could see Ed with half his head severed by a blow of his favorite sculpture. In spite of that, the peace overshadowed, and I felt protected.

After a few moments, the love in my heart welled up more, and I found myself whispering, "I give you my love. I give you my heart." I don't know how long I thought those words before it dawned on me what I was thinking.

I could feel love go out. I know it sounds crazy, but I felt like a generator of energy. I could actually feel something being sent out, presumably to him.

In the distance, like another world, I heard periodically "Homo, homo," and "You fucking faggot," along with the slamming of the door. My response was not fear this time. I just continued whispering, "I give you my love. I give you my heart."

Almost subconsciously, the words changed. I was saying, "I receive your love. I receive your heart." It didn't make sense to my logical mind. "This man has no love, no heart," the static in my head argued. "There is nothing to receive."

"Oh, yes," a gentle part of me reminded. "We are all love. That can't be changed. We are made in the image of God, and we are love. The jock might be denying that right now, but he has a soul, a Higher Self, and that is love. Regardless of his actions, he is love, and his Higher Self can easily send that to you."

My head felt like Grand Central Station. My mind doubted with a furry. The gentle rebuttal spoke softly, while the four short sentences impulsed over and over.

"I give you my love. I give you my heart. I receive your love. I receive your heart. I give you my love. I give you my heart. I receive your love. I receive your heart. ..."

I knew intuitively that some part of him could hear me and was responding. I could feel the energy I was generating go out, and I could feel his energy come back to me. The two met in a swirl, of sorts, while I just sat there, basking in the sensation.

I completely lost touch with time. It may have been three minutes or thirty, but before long, the hollering stopped. I continued the four sentences, and I really did feel a love for him, a oneness, even a slight affection.

When it became obvious the trauma was over, I just sat there mulling over—not the hollering—but rather this new-found knowledge. It all started making sense. For years I had accepted as fact that I am responsible for everything I experience. Had I thought about it, I'm sure it would have been hard to figure out exactly why I had brought about such a traumatic evening. However, I didn't have to think. As I sat there I could see what I had done. I realized I had set up a situation so I could learn and test this new knowledge in one big swoop.

I had experienced and learned the art of giving and receiving love. It did indeed melt the problem, just like they taught in Sunday school. I was thunderstruck, and don't believe I got another wink of sleep. I had experienced that giving and receiving love is truly turning on a light to dispel darkness. It really worked.

Since that evening I have experienced these four sentences in many situations. They never let me down.

I saw the jock only one more time. Two days later I met him on our common driveway when he had to back up his car for me. I quickly said the four sentences, since I felt uneasy running into him. As I passed, he smiled, and we waved as if nothing had happened. No doubt that would have happened anyway, since we've all felt foolish for the things we did when we were two sheets to the wind. At any rate, the love those words generated for me changed my whole experience of him as we waved each other past. I wasn't afraid of him, nor angry, nor intimidated. I felt whole, confident, and loving, and I'm sure I showed it. I knew these sentences were to be very significant in my life.

In this spirexual experience, there are only four words to remember: *LOVE*, and *HEART*, and *GIVE*, and *RECEIVE*. Simply visualize someone and think the four sentences. *"I give you my love. I give you my heart. I receive your love. I receive your heart."*

You can think these in the depths of meditation, or frantic moments of peril, as I did. Neither special time nor preparation is required. Just the thought of the four sentences with someone in mind does the trick.

If you choose someone you're bothered by, the roughness quickly smooths out. If you choose someone you truly do love—and, yes, these words are wonderful for them too—the feeling intensifies.

The Cape Cod summer ended about a month later, and I was once again saddled with the emotions of letting go of my ten year relationship. I decided to go to Santa Fe, since it is one of my favorite cities. My soon-to-be-ex was at our Laguna Beach home and made it clear he didn't want me there.

I found the perfect apartment in Santa Fe with a stunning view of downtown, the capitol, the Ortiz Mountains, a sliver of the Rockies, and the famous New Mexican adobe architecture in the foreground.

I felt like I had gone to heaven, but my heart still ached for my lover. I wanted so much to hold him, if not to make love to him. I would call, only to get more emotional while trying to show him I didn't care, was completely recovered, and quite stable. Nothing was farther from the truth. One night while laying in a lonely bed, those four sentences came to me. I visualized him and repeated the words. The pain eased. I felt his presence. The same feeling I had when we cuddled returned. Eureka!! At long last I felt I might be able to get a handle on the heartbreak and distress I was experiencing.

I can't honestly say that all my pain immediately vanished, never to return. But, it did become manageable. Furthermore, I felt like I was again loving him. With these words I was telling him how I felt. Somehow I knew he could hear me and was responding. I just knew it.

Quite frankly, I suppose my child within thought these words would bring him back. Some of my peace of mind may have come from those fantasies. That wasn't to be, but he did get my message. Energy is actually sent with these four sentences. Shortly after I started saying these words to him, I got a letter. It was full of love. "I've been thinking about you a lot lately," he said, not to my surprise. Of course, he still wanted his "freedom." Even that began to seem okay now that I could truly still experience love with him.

I am absolutely convinced that energy is sent with these four sentences. Often, quite often, the person will think of you in a loving way. I've had friends call me after I thought the words. "I had the strongest urge to see how you're doing," they would say, and I knew why.

This spirexual experience I call *The Love Meltdown*. It is precious, powerful, and will melt mountains of distress. I shared this experience with a group of gay men and lesbians at the Unity Church in Seattle. The next day I ran into one of the men. He was a cook at the restaurant where a friend and I had dinner, and he made a point of coming out to tell us how he had to use these words several times that day. People seemed to be at cross purposes with him, but when he silently thought the words, the tenseness eased. I could not help but think how fortunate he was to set up those situations so he could also test and learn the knowledge in one big swoop.

These words are for our own growth. However, we can act in concert to change the world. As a group, our thoughts are incredibly effective. The power of a group thinking these words of giving and receiving love together at the same time under one roof is found by squaring the number of people. Six is the same as thirty six people thinking alone. One hundred is the same as ten thousand. Two hundred is forty thousand.

This is the law of nature Maharishi explains when he brings thousands together to promote world enlightenment. The harmonic convergence ceremonies recognized this also. Another group organizes an annual world peace vigil where people congregate around the globe at the same time. Earth day is the same principle.

Because of this law of nature, we can enlighten world leaders about any topic on which there is widespread ignorance, such as homosexuality, environmental pollution, social freedoms, and racial tension. We simply think *The Love Meltdown* in a group with the intention that Truth about some certain subject ride on the waves of love we're generating.

Acid really stings until it is neutralized by a basic solution. Our basic solution is love. Love is really the basic ingredient in creation, and love is *the* solution. So, we can neutralize some of the ignorance held by some of the people who misunderstand or who harbor some prejudice with the basic solution of love.

We don't have to plant new thoughts in anyone's head. Truth is already there. We simply need to give them a chance to see and feel the Truth more clearly. We do this by using the power of a group and simply thinking together these four sentences with the intention to neutralize some specific ignorance. Everything else is automatic. There's nothing else to do or say. Just silently think and feel together the four simple sentences.

The group *Love Meltdown* is quite easy. The leader tells everyone to close their eyes and leads them through the thoughts. At one meeting of gay men and lesbians our object was to change world understanding of homosexuals. I started by saying, "Now visualize the Supreme Court of the United States and think *I give you my love, I give you my heart."* I paused for a few moments, then continued, "Now think *I receive your love, I receive your heart.* Think these words once, then back off and wallow in the love that wells up from within."

After one minute I gave the same instruction for the President, Vice President, and cabinet to be visualized together. After another minute, I gave the instruction for our elected lawmakers in a joint session of Congress. Then I told them to visualize religious leaders of the world in a large

19

auditorium, followed by a gathering of television, radio, and newspaper executives and reporters.

In my presentations to gay men and lesbians, the object is to send love to melt misunderstanding about homosexuality. All we need is the intention—an ever so faint intention—that the people open up to the Truth. We don't have to dwell on it, just know that is what we are doing. Our intentions are more powerful than we can imagine.

The unifying force of love is so strong that it will expose Truth. Those individuals and groups we visualize with *The Love Meltdown* will have "ah-ha" experiences. There will be breakthroughs in their thinking. And the best part is that they will give themselves credit for figuring it out on their very own. If we proselytized, they would probably resist and close up even more. Love cracks hard shells.

When I share this experience with an audience, I often use current events that need an infusion of Truth and love, such as summit conferences, social unrest, wars, natural disasters, and accidents. Before I was introduced to one group, the chairman told them that one of their women members had been beaten and stabbed to death the night before. When we experienced together *The Love Meltdown,* I added a section for the slain person. We all gave her love and heart, and we all received her love and heart. No-one in that room could deny the power of these words. We all felt her presence and a strong connection.

These four words can change the world. We can, in our silent unobtrusive way, change human awareness about ourselves, the environment, or any other misunderstood topic, by expanding the influence of love in this way.

These four sentences are incredibly powerful. They can be used in thousands of different situations. Let your imagination be your guide.


### THE LOVE MELTDOWN
*Giving And Receiving Love And Heart*

*Visualize one or more people and think with feeling these four sentences:*
*I give you my love;*
*I give you my heart;*
*I receive your love;*
*I receive your heart.*

CHAPTER FOUR

## *Gay Or Non-Gay In The Image Of God*

I can never doubt the perfection of my being gay. I know that my sexual activities have not hampered my spiritual growth. Of course, I have had lots of sexual trips that would raise an eyebrow or two. At times, even my parent's Victorian views crept in to make me wonder, "Hey, Roger, is this right?"

I need only think of my growth from the context of sex to know the answer. The trauma behind discovering *The Love Meltdown* is an example. My being gay was the issue, and it led to a greater appreciation of love. Sexuality was the backdrop for that lesson, and I am truly grateful for the experience.

In 1974 I had another spiritual experience centering around sex. I remember reading for the umpteenth time those marvelous books my music teacher gave me. I'm sure she had loaned them to me, but twenty eight years later I still had them. I sat on our deck in Laguna Beach overlooking the ocean, Catalina Island, and the beautiful town below. I read that we can do anything we want, we just need to know it. "I know I can," I thought, "but I still feel so limited. There must be something else." I said a short prayer asking that I be shown what else to do.

I forgot that moment, only to reconstruct these events years later. About two weeks after the

22

prayer I went to the Corral Club. This was a popular gay bath in Los Angeles. My lover and I had a liberal arrangement, as did nearly everyone we knew. He would drop me off at the baths, then go to the bars, returning around two in the morning for the ride back to Laguna Beach to exchange stories about what happened. At least twice a month we did that, and it seemed perfectly natural at the time. Our gay social structure has changed now, and I feel almost embarrassed to publicly admit our habits.

As soon as I walked into the Corral Club that evening, I saw Jim. He had a brightness and radiated an essence I couldn't resist. We smiled in the hall, but he immediately linked up with another person. "Oh well, win some, loose some," I thought. We got rather philosophical at the baths in those days.

A couple of hours later I saw Jim again, and this time he was more receptive. We went into a small room to have sex, but never did. Instead we held hands and touched, while he told me why he was so full of brightness. He had just finished a weekend retreat for people practicing Transcendental Meditation. I learned all about TM for the first time and was quite intrigued.

The next week Jim and his lover invited me to West Los Angeles for dinner. It turned out that his lover was a TM teacher and was teaching at the TM center the next Saturday. Without hesitation I signed up and was initiated. This was my first journey inward. I now realize there are many paths leading to the peace within, but I have a special gratitude for the first one to come into my life. Before the year expired I was in Switzerland for training to be a TM teacher myself.

What a milestone it was to meet Jim. And that milestone took place in the baths!! If there is any place we can be judgmental about gay sex, it would be the baths. Yet it was the backdrop for the answer to my prayer. Sitting in the Corral Club I renewed the spiritual journey I'm still on. My sexual attraction to Jim changed my whole life—not by dropping gay sex, but by adding the dimension of spirit.

It is not unusual for our sexual experiences to be intertwined with our most meaningful spiritual breakthroughs. These attractions play a significant role for every person on earth in their spiritual awakening, and it matters not how that attraction is expressed. I'm grateful that my own sexual orientation led me to my mentors so I could discover my Self.

And what have I discovered? I have come to understand that I really am made in the image of God—one of my first lessons in Sunday school after a night of love with my third grade lover. That phrase, *in the image of God,* seems to imply that God is a being like us, having a body and living someplace out there. That's not an accurate picture, though one commonly held. Even to use the word *God* runs the risk of that picture creeping in.

God is greater than the greatest you can imagine—greater than all of creation. And God is smaller than the smallest—smaller than the most elementary particle in the atom. God is infinite energy and also absolute silence. That being the case, He/She is beyond our intellectual understanding. We can't fathom the unfathomable, but we can experience Him/Her.

That's easy to do because we are made in His/Her image. Take that literally. All of the qualities God has, He/She gave to us. God could not do otherwise, any more than you could give your child less than what you have.

The concept of Mother/Father God is easier for me to grasp when I think in terms of nature. Everything in nature is a manifestation of some aspect of God. The many types of trees and leaves, the insects, the birds, the fish, the mammals, the rocks and soil, the water, the clouds, the planets, the stars, the galaxies. The list would go on forever. That is nature, and all of that represents God's body.

But God is more than a body—more than the greatest. That more is *Spirit*. It is this Spirit that is our connection to God, for it is the same Spirit that is ours.

Spirit—our Spirit, God's Spirit—has all the qualities of God. And all of us are one with that Spirit. That is, each of us is that spirit—totally. We are individual and unique, but at the same moment we own all the Spirit is and has.

While we are in a physical body, we seem to be limited in space and time. That is the nature of the physical, and we have chosen to experience this time and this space. That choice of ours does not in the slightest bit cut away what we truly are in Spirit. It only locks us in to certain experiences. So, while we are here on earth now, we are still Spirit, and it is our Spirit that is made in the image of Mother/Father God.

Notice the structure of this divine truth: *We are made in the image of God.* It's in the present tense. It says we are now in the image of God. It says God made us in His/Her image now. The act is completed. We are completely made in the image of God now.

That means we don't need to evolve, or go through a myriad of lessons, for we are all now, in this moment, already perfectly evolved. With infinite love, God could not make us to suffer through hell to finally reach bliss. No! He/She made us in bliss in His/Her image, and what we decide to do with our experiences is up to us. God won't interfere. He/She doesn't need to. We have everything, including all-knowing intelligence, so there is nothing else God needs to do for us.

Furthermore, just because some of us have chosen to be miserable, does not make us any less perfect, or less divine, or less a Spirit. We are all perfection now.

Even as Spirits we are unique and individual. In this particular incarnation we are even more individualized. Take, for instance, the issue of gender. The Spirit is androgynous—both male and female. The Spirit has all the receptive and nurturing energies of the female, and the Spirit also has all the creative and dominant energies of the male. When we take on a body to lock ourselves into the *here and now*, we choose to emphasize one gender or the other. It's like taking money out of the bank when we go on a trip. The cash is with us, but we still have the rest of our money elsewhere in a safe place. Some of us decided we would play with our male nature. Others are playing with the female nature. The most masculine red neck truck driver also has a feminine nature in his Spirit, even though it might still be in the *bank back at home.*

The same goes for sexuality. At the Spirit level we are totally sexual and asexual. The whole spectrum is present. When we come into this world we can bring whatever part of our sexuality we decide is best for the experiences we want. Therefore the combinations of our gender and sexuality are several:

male with attraction to female;
male with attraction to male;
male with attraction to male and female;
female with attraction to male;
female with attraction to female;
female with attraction to male and female.

Each of these combinations is valid. Each has its basis in Spirit. Each reflects some aspect of our whole Self. Each is exactly what we wanted to draw out of the bank for this glorious trip to planet earth. And most importantly, each is in the image of God. Everyone is male or female with sexual attractions, and everyone is in the image of God. Yes, we are gay or non-gay in the image of God.

To say Martha is made lesbian in the image of God is not to say God is lesbian. Remember, God is greater than the greatest, and that includes His/Her attractions. That attraction is more than gay, more than non-gay, and it includes both.

For some reason humans do not readily accept their divine qualities. They'll repeat and repeat that humankind is made in God's image, but they have a difficult time realizing they each have the same qualities as God. That can only mean they doubt they are made in the image of God.

This gets us to the next spirexual experience, *Our Creator Connection.* In this simple experience, we think of all of the qualities we would give God, and then we claim them for ourselves. Think of God as being all of the nature around us, and all creative forces of nature, and more. Don't isolate Him/Her as a being.

When you claim His/Her qualities as your own, think of your Self as Spirit, the same Spirit that is God. We share God's Spirit with Him/Her and with each other, like we share the air we breath with the sky and with each other.

What are some of the qualities you would give God? Think of some. God is love. God is light. God is happiness, joy, and bliss. God is all-knowing intelligence. God is everywhere present. God is perfection. God is peace and gentleness. God is infinite energy. God is abundance. God is without judgment. God is timeless.

Then claim these qualities for your Self. They are yours. I am love. I am light. I am happiness, joy, and bliss. I am all-knowing intelligence. I am everywhere present. I am perfection. I am peace and gentleness. I am infinite energy. I am abundance. I am without judgment. I am timeless.

I believe we can also include the qualities of sensual, and sexually uninhibited, and androgynous, and lesbian, and gay, and non-gay. We can locate God's qualities by looking at our own qualities. We are full, unique Spirits made in God's image and with a special expression of God's qualities on earth now. God is infinitely diverse with an infinite variety of unique parts. So are we. What we have chosen to bring with us on this earth trip gives us our human individuality. And, all those wonderful qualities we have chosen for our uniqueness are also qualities of Spirit, of God.

We must be careful not to include the *empty qualities* when we experience *Our Creator Connection.* They really only describe the absence of a God-quality. Sadness is the absence of happiness. Poverty is the absence of abundance. Turmoil is the absence of peace. We want only to emphasize our fullness, not the emptiness.

Make a habit to think your God qualities every day, perhaps in the morning before getting up or at night before going to sleep. Think them also when you need centering, you feel some roughness, or you're faced with a challenge. In these words are grand impulses of energy that can change your life.

Yes, we are gay and non-gay in the image of Mother/Father God, and let's not forget that. We have all the power with us to do anything we set out to do. We don't have to overcome our sexuality, or go celibate, or give up any form of love in our lives. We are already perfect.

## OUR CREATOR CONNECTION
### *Claiming God's Qualities*
### *As Your Own*

*Think of some of Mother/Father God's qualities:*
> God is love.
> God is light.
> God is happiness, joy, and bliss.
> God is all-knowing intelligence.
> God is everywhere present.
> God is perfection.
> God is peace and gentleness.
> God is infinite energy.
> God is abundance.
> God is without judgment.
> God is timeless.

*Then claim these qualities for your Self:*
> I am love.
> I am light.
> I am happiness, joy, and bliss.
> I am all-knowing intelligence.
> I am everywhere present.
> I am perfection.
> I am peace and gentleness.
> I am infinite energy.
> I am without judgment.
> I am timeless.

# CHAPTER FIVE

## *Love*

I truly loved Santa Fe, but there was deep loneliness. Frequently I wondered if being single was my path to Self-sufficiency. This is not an unusual idea, I've found. Many of my friends suggest the notion that wanting a lover is like wanting a crutch.

I now believe that is not the case. Being mated or bonding with a best friend is natural. Whether the bonding is with a best friend or a lover depends on your goals this in lifetime. Neither is preferred, but some kind of special connection with someone is important. That is so we can experience *oneness*, because feeling love is really feeling the most elementary level of creation. But I'm getting ahead of my story. More on that later.

I knew I wanted a live-in mate. That's my style, and I discovered in Santa Fe that finding the perfect person is as simple as the four simple sentences: *I give you my love; I give you my heart; I receive your love; I receive your heart.* I said them with the intention they be routed to the perfect person without laying down any preconceived conditions. And I believed they were being routed to him, and I believed he would respond at a subconscious level. I had no person in mind, only the vision he be perfect for me. I knew that great forces of nature were at work for the two of us to meet.

31

Although the words and procedure are the same as *The Love Meltdown*, I call this *The Love Handle*. Like the other spirexual experiences, *The Love Handle* is extremely simple, and it does work. However, you must intend it for a perfect person without conditions, and you must believe the process is happening.

I did intend, and I did believe, and the fateful day did arrive. I woke up with the strongest urge to drive to the hot springs, about two hours into the mountains. I bounced out of bed, grabbed some mushy bananas I got on sale, some tahini, and a package of rice cakes, and I drove off. There was a sense of excitement, but then the natural, clear hot pools overlooking a red rock canyon is one of my favorite places in New Mexico.

I parked the car, headed down the steep snow packed incline, across the river on a fallen log, and up a muddy slope. Panting for breath, my first sight was Drew, stark naked, eating tortilla chips and refried beans.

"Hi" was my breathless introduction. He didn't look up. His friend was receptive, however. We chatted while I undressed. A silent Drew just ate his chips. Then I went into the main pool while they hiked up to another spring. I remember being disappointed, because I was so attracted to something about Drew, although he was more lanky than my usual type.

An hour later they returned, and Drew sat next to me in the spring. We broke the ice. He was traveling from North Carolina to California—just to see it. No plans, no particular destination. Just California. He had met the other fellow the night before and delayed his trip west to see these springs. He had never been to a hot spring before.

"Don't you dare go on before visiting Santa Fe," I insisted. "It's one of the country's most interesting and beautiful cities." He was still anxious to get on to California.

In my animation, or perhaps attraction, one of my gestures nicked his arm. Drew grew nervous, because unbeknownst to me he was afraid of an erection. He quickly moved across the small pool. I crumbled inside, but not enough to withhold my last question.

"When's your birthday?" I asked. I figured he ought to get used to California type questions.

The 18th," he answered.

"Of what?"

"August."

"You have to be kidding." I was thunderstruck. "That's my birthday too."

Drew finally came to life. Although we kept our distance, we did finally start talking. I can keep a conversation moving when I want to, and something told me I wanted to.

Before I left for home, I scratched my phone number on a paper and handed it to Drew. "In case you change your mind, I have a spare bedroom."

The next day Drew did show up in Santa Fe. I showed him the historical district, and we rode into the Rockies. The next day we hiked down to the Rio Grande. That February afternoon was quite comfortable. We took off our clothes and sunbathed on a sheet while I told him some of the sights to visit in California.

Suddenly—and I mean suddenly—we both felt a rush of bliss in our hearts. We looked at each other.

"You feel that?"

"I think so."

Without words, we moved closer together, touched, lightly kissed, then embraced.

"My God," I thought, "how can this be? I'm feeling so much love. Am I falling in love? With him? Are these feeling coming from him? Or from me?"

At that moment the picture got clearer. Somehow the love which I could feel had brought us together. He had come all the way from North Carolina. I was guided to go the hot springs. We were to meet. And as we held each other I could feel that love.

Drew kept delaying his departure for California. Finally I went with him in April. Then he took me to North Carolina while he finished school. That was three years ago, and we're still together.

Many of my friends with whom I have shared *The Love Handle* have experienced results. A couple of weeks ago I got a phone call from half way around the world. A woman wanted to know precisely "what those four magic sentences are." Her friend Suzanne had just moved to Europe to be with a new husband. I had seen Suzanne only six months earlier when she was recovering from the pangs of loneliness and divorce. I shared the words with her, and evidently she gave them credit for her new husband. For some reason, however, she was reluctant to pass on the knowledge; I hope you won't be.

Drew's and my fateful meeting and our feelings at the Rio Grande set into motion a quest to explain love. Using the channeling tools you will develop in a few more chapters, I learned love is none other than the most elementary energy in creation.

Layer by layer science has stripped away the distinctions between the multifarious substances and energies of creation. Scientists first isolated the natural elements, then reduced these to a few fundamental particles. Ultimately everything boiled down to space, time, matter, energy, and gravitation.

In his General Relativity, Einstein showed that space and time are a continuum. In his Special Relativity, he showed that matter and energy are the same. Gravity appeared to have no relationship with the other four, and Einstein couldn't fathom that. His Unified Field Theory states that everything in the universe—gravitational force, electromagnetic force, matter and energy, electric charge and field, space and time—fades into a very simple underlying reality. They merge into one, so the underlying unity of the universe is laid bare.

Well, Einstein is right. The unified field does exist. It is none other than love. Love is the basis of everything and everyone in creation. Even more remarkable, is that we are made to feel that love, the fundamental basis of all, the unified field.

We have all experienced love in our hearts—the gentle pulsation of creation. It is in our hearts that we are connected to all of creation. It is in our hearts that we feel the connection to each other.

*The Love Meltdown* and *The Love Handle* take on special meaning now. *I give you my love. I give you my heart. I receive your love. I receive your heart.* By giving and receiving our hearts, we open the floodgates for love to flow. Heart is an essential ingredient in those two spirexual experiences. Heart is the physical vehicle for us to feel love flow from and to each other—indeed from and to every being in all of creation.

Opening our hearts brings the feeling of love flowing. It is remarkable enough that we are part of the mechanical flow of love, but even more remarkable is that we can actually feel it. We are conscious of it. That means no less than we are conscious of the flow of creation!! Think about it. Our wonderful nervous system can actually give us the experience of feeling the flow of the life blood of everything in all of creation.

It brings with it much more than the feelings, though. It brings all the energy and intelligence of nature. It brings all of God's qualities, not just to be there in the abstract, but to know, sense, feel, experience, and have them for our own use.

As if by piggy-back, all of God's qualities— indeed all of nature's attributes—hitch a ride on that energy of love which we feel in our hearts. It can't be any other way, because everything else is made of love also. Wherever there is love, there is the potential for anything. And conversely, whenever there is anything, even the smallest subatomic particle, there is love and with it the potential for all of God's qualities.

Love in its most refined state is that simple, easy, sweet energy we feel pulsating in our open hearts. It is that pulsation in the heart region we zero in on for *The Conscious Connection.*

When love stirs, new energies result. When these energies stir, the whole spectrum of creation can manifest. So, within love are all the opposite and infinite variations of our world: hard rock and water; flat leaves and chunky trunks; fish that swim and birds that fly; the bitter and the sweet; the light and the dark; the loud and the silent; elephants and virus; giraffes and snails; and on and on and on.

Each human is noticeably very unique and special. We each look different. We each have different talents. We each have different philosophies. We each seem to have our own unique approach to sex, far beyond the broad distinctions of being gay or non-gay. All of our many differences illustrate the wonderful diversity of life.

These are all expressions of that same love. So, while different, everything is *ONE*—that one energy that packs with it all the infinite qualities of nature, of God.

This is the unified field of Einstein. No wonder then that all the great religions of the world agree on at least on basic Truth: *God is love.* No wonder then that *We are love.* These aren't just religious doctrines. These really are scientific principles. Science and spirituality are saying the same thing.

So when you think the four simple sentences of *The Love Meltdown* and the *The Love Handle,* feel what is really happening. By giving our love and heart, we open our channel for this energy to flow. It is slippery. It slips and slides all over everything. Nothing can contain it, and of course, we do feel it.

When a physicist super-cools a substance to nearly absolute zero (so cold that all molecular motion stops), the substance takes on that same slippery quality of the love in our hearts. It slips right through its container, becomes super viscous, and easily permeates everything around it. That is love, of course, in one of its simplest physical forms.

When we open ourselves to receive someone else's heart and love, our love quickly slips through space and time to activate a direct energy link between the two of us. That link is always there. It has to be there because everything is made of love and everything is connected by love.

Being conscious of love is key to our spiritual growth. When we are aware of something, we can use it. A stove is worthless to us if it is locked behind enclosed cupboards and we don't know it's there. Open the cupboard, turn on the burner, and presto, we're cooking with gas. It's that way with love. It's always there, but when we *feel* it, we can use all it represents—none less than all the forces of nature. *Feel* is the key. When we feel the love in our lives, we can have all the knowledge, support, abundance, and joy of nature because all of God's qualities are there. However, we must *feel* the love.

That is why love and sex are intertwined. It is no mere accident of words that we say, "I want to make love to you." Sex is one way to feel love.

In my early days of spiritual awakening, I assumed sex was somehow mortal. I wanted to become immortal, and I thought sex was a barrier. I longed for the time when I became so Christ-like that sex would drop off. It never dawned on me what a powerful tool that sex is for experiencing God, for experiencing creation, for experiencing love.

I now realize that sex is a divine expression of God's love. It is a spiritual experience in itself. It can bring the feeling of being unified—not just with your partner, but with all of creation. In that context, sex is divinely holy. It is a step toward going home. So, while we're in a physical body, let's make love in every way we know how, and that includes physical sex.

At the University of North Carolina the Carolina Gay and Lesbian Association sponsored a panel discussion with Youth For Christ about homosexuality and religion. A wide range of religious views were present with many pastors, including a Baptist, supporting a positive attitude on gay and lesbian sex. The more fundamental view, however, emphasized that gay sex is unChristian, and certainly unnatural. One minister latched onto the concept that the missionary position is the only sexual embrace, and he could conceive of only a man and a woman in that union expressing God's love. Another pastor even felt the intention to conceive was necessary to feel the love.

That narrow view of love is not true. In all forms of sexual expression, we can and do experience love, simply because we all are love, and we can and do experience our own essence. The non-gays certainly do feel beauty and love with their partners. My experience is clearly that gay men and lesbians do also.

I asked one of the ministers what he thought Jesus would say today about homosexuality. He said it doesn't matter because Jesus set up a church to make these moral guidelines. Wasn't it the church that tried to isolate and silence those who dared to suggest the earth isn't the center of the universe? Jesus was—and still is—a living example of love personified, and the distorted views of his teachings can not alter my love and affection for him. By the time you have experienced and regularly practiced all these spirexual techniques, you will know first hand from him and many other Masters that sex can be a path toward Self realization, whether or not the sex is gay, lesbian, or non-gay.

This leads us to the next spirexual experience: *The Love Connection.* This is almost too simple to be labeled a technique, yet we need somehow to be reminded about its power. When you are with someone special, focus on the feeling of love. *Feel* love. It's your feeling. It doesn't come from the other person, but your partner is a catalyst for the feeling. Get completely immersed in the feeling, knowing you are feeling the unified field, the most elementary energy in creation. Just let it be.

We can use all our sexual encounters to enliven our feelings of love. Then sex is truly divinely holy.

It helps, of course, to act tenderly. Gently kiss and caress. Feel him or her all over. Slowly undress. Speak of love—don't be afraid to express this love feeling. You don't have to frighten you partner with *I love you,* but speak of the beauty you see or your appreciation of a special presence. Pick out something that is truly wonderful and bellow it out. Mutual admiration is an aspect of love. Use it freely.

The key words are: *focus, feel,* and *express.* Then let the love well up. It brings with it enlightenment and all the gifts of God. Know that what you are doing is good and can only lead to good when you focus on that feeling of love. Regardless of your sexual orientation, these principles are the same.

In every encounter with another person, we can have *The Love Connection.* It can be sexual, but it doesn't have to be. All of us are love. We are all connected. We are all different. Using this spirexual experience, we can all unify with someone in love.


## THE LOVE HANDLE
### Attracting A Perfect Person

*Think these four simple sentences with the intention they be routed to the perfect person as your lover or friend, and with the belief the process is arranging to bring the two of you together:*

> *I give you my love;*
> *I give you my heart;*
> *I receive your love;*
> *I receive your heart.*


## THE LOVE CONNECTION
### Focusing Love On Another

*Focus on love with someone in mind. Express love silently and out loud. Get Completely immersed in the feeling, knowing you are feeling the most elementary energy in creation.*

# CHAPTER SIX

## *Forgiveness*

Our understanding of love is fundamental for our understanding of forgiveness. When the connection between forgiveness and love dawned on me, it changed my life. I am sure it will yours also.

We start with the basic Truth we now know about love: it is the most elementary energy in creation. Everything and everyone is made of love, and God is love. All of nature is simply different expressions of that same basic love energy, and we are capable of experiencing and feeling that most subtle aspect of God's creation.

All of humankind's creations are also love—our buildings, cars, clothes, factories, even chemicals, guns, and bombs. Nothing can exist that is not from that basic elementary energy that Einstein called *The Unified Field*.

Our bodies are made of love. Our Higher Self is also love. Love is the slippery thread that connects all of us with every other being in creation.

Even more remarkable than this very simple understanding of a complex creation, is that we are made to feel that love. What this means is that we are able to tune into our true nature. In more esoteric circles they say the observer discovers he is the observed. What we observe then is that everything is an aspect of our Self.

This is because whatever we observe has that same basic indivisible energy of love for its building block as we do.

In Eastern philosophy this is what is meant by *I am that.* Yes, you can literally observe another person and say, "I am that." Or you can look at a tree and say, "I am that." Or you can marvel at a tide pool and think, "I am that." Or you can gaze into the night sky and whisper, "I am that."

The realization that we are love and that everything else is also love personalizes the impersonal world. We never intentionally would hurt our own Self—at least not without a distorted outlook. The psychotic can try to kill himself or inflict serious body injury on himself, and we all recognize that as serious mental derangement. We understand the person doesn't see reality quite right.

Yet, humans kill whole species of animals for sport or reckless harvesting. We send acid and smog into our air. We pour chemicals into our rivers and lakes. We kill each other in the name of religion, or territory, or money.

We humans do not consider ourselves mentally deranged when we intentionally harm our environment or even kill other people in war. In reality, we are inflicting Self injury in all these situations. We can not ever harm the smallest plant without feeling it on our soul level, because we are one with and connected to that plant. I am not speaking of using plants or animals for food, because all of creation is to be used for our nourishment and growth. I am speaking of the intentional infliction of needless suffering for no particular purpose on our environment and its life forms.

We can't put filth into our world without putting filth into our own Selves, because we share the soul of love with all that is around us. We can't hurt another human without it being a Self inflicted wound. All the cries of nature, the screams of slain soldiers, the yelping of tortured animals reverberate throughout the cosmos, just as the song of the whale is heard under water around the world.

We are in a sea of love. We are individual expressions within that sea, but the sea is our foundation. Whatever we do to the foundation will surely affect the structure of our life.

When we all realize *WE ARE THAT*, then we will will quickly stop all this Self infliction. This is our goal as enlightened people.

We homosexuals often feel we are the objects of prejudice, scorn, ridicule, and even torture and violence. This is so much a part of our experience that most of us hide, like the newborn fish hide in the grasses to keep from being eaten. We deny our sexuality to all but a select few; even many of our parents are not privy to this information. We are indeed scared to let other people know who we are and how we love.

Why? For good reason. Out there are fellow humans hurting their own Selves by their deranged acts and thoughts about homosexuality. They have sent tons of negative garbage into our sea of love, and we all feel it. We know its there in that *mass-consciousness*. As children we could sense it, even without the slightest experience of it yet. Few children need to learn that being gay or a lesbian is something that must be kept quiet. They pick it up from the ether around them. I certainly did.

All of nature constantly tries to right what humankind has wronged. We deforest a range, and nature tries to grow it back. We foul the air, and nature tries to purge and clean. We wound another person's flesh, and nature tries to heal. We constantly marvel at the power of nature and her persistence in bringing back balance, regardless of our continuing assaults upon her. This is the power of love. Love is nature. That sea of love has all the qualities of Mother/Father God and can do anything. It simply needs to be given half a chance.

Actually, it needs less than that. The power of love is so great that only a small bit neutralizes tons of negative influence. This is the power behind the group spirexual experience of *The Love Meltdown*. We can begin the process of bringing balance back to earth. If only we gay men, lesbians, and enlightened heterosexuals did this, balance would return, so powerful is this influence.

We can bring balance back simply with *The Love Meltdown* as individuals and groups. It has its effect because *we are that* and *they are that*. When we enliven *that* we forever change to some degree what everyone perceives. Eventually, we all perceive ourselves as love, as connected, as whole, and as One.

Another way we do this is by the act of forgiveness. This is much simpler than most people realize because forgiveness is misunderstood. To understand forgiveness, just remember that all of creation is made of love, and we are made to receive that love. That is what life is for: to receive creation's love. However, life isn't just for receiving love. Life is also for giving love to everyone and everything.

This little Truth unlocks easy forgiving. *Life is for giving love.* "For giving." "For giving" love. That is forgiveness. It's just giving love. Nothing more.

When we hold grudges, we are choosing to withhold that sweet taste of love we can give. Get rid of that grudge, and once gain your life is "for giving" love.

Grudges are really easy to release once we realize what a silly illusion they are. We hold grudges because we think someone has hurt us. We imagine we have been trespassed, compromised, attacked, or in some way made a lesser person. Such folly! We made in the image of God. We are perfection, and no-one, nothing, can alter that.

In the past when we have forgiven, we have thought something like this: "You have done a wrong to me, but I don't want to hold a grudge, so I am going to try to forget that terrible thing you did."

Such words recognize an illusion. They give power to a mistake: that anyone could harm us without our consent. It is impossible. We are creators because we have all the attributes of our creator, and He/She is a creator. No-one can interfere with our creation without our consent, even though we may not be hearing that consent. Our own creation begins with our thoughts and we must take responsibility for what we think. Thoughts are the beginning of our experience.

That's why it is so very important we think correctly about homosexuality. If we don't, no-one else will. When we do, we alter the sea of mass-consciousness to neutralize homophobia. Furthermore, as we change our own thinking, we change our own experiences. Only then will we be able to be openly gay men and lesbians to experience love and support from everyone in the world.

The first step is to forgive using *The Forgiveness Formula,* our next spirexual experience. Instead of forgiving in that old mode, we just give love. That is the total act of forgiveness: giving love. When you feel a grudge against anyone whom you think has trespassed against you or hurt you in any way, think the substance of these words:

*"I have made a mistake in my thinking to allow you to seemingly hurt me. I recognize that you are merely doing what I invited, and that in reality neither you nor anyone else can hurt me. I am perfect now, always have been, and always will be. You can't change that. I now recognize that life is for giving love to you."*

An abbreviated version of these forgiving words can be:

*"I send you love from my heart, and I forgive you, knowing it is impossible for you to infringe on my perfection."*

In this spirexual experience of forgiveness, don't restrict yourselves by giving love to just those who bother you. Also give love to those you truly do love, often and unsolicited. You can do this by thinking:

*"I send you love from my heart."*

Forgiveness is a marvelous way to go to sleep at night. Our thoughts before sleep can improve our rest and mental processing, and thoughts of love are the highest possible. When you're going to sleep, just think of people that flash into your awareness and think "I give you my love."

Giving love changes the consciousness of the receiver. You can't put honey on a woman's tongue and not have her taste it. When you send love energy, it actually permeates your recipients, whether or not they are aware of it. With it comes a degree of insight, peace, vitality, and optimism. One infusion won't change their world completely, but it does make a difference, and it does build up. It is really a gift to ourselves when we unload grudges and infuse God's qualities around us. All of this happens silently and automatically, without confrontation or explanation.

*The Love Meltdown* is another form of forgiveness. You can use it instead of these other suggestions, or you can dream up one of your very own. The only important point is that giving love alone is the act of forgiveness. Nothing else needs to be thought. You don't need to recreate or harp on any situation. You don't need to communicate your forgiveness to the other person. And you don't need to forget either. You simply give love. And when you do, all tensions spontaneously cease. If the tensions return, again give love.

A corollary to this spirexual experience is to randomly give love to people who pass by you. You do this silently to friends, strangers, fellow workers, or whomsoever you're around. This is such a simple thing, and one day all of mankind will understand its power and significance.

We now have another way to start changing the world. We just need to remember that life is for giving love, and then to give love to those who bother us and to those we truly do love.

## THE FORGIVENESS FORMULA
### Sending Love And Recognizing
### There Is Nothing To Forgive

*Recognize that life is "for giving" love and then generously give that love. As often as the urge comes, silently say to those around you or those you visualize (regardless of your relationship to them):*

*"My heart is for giving love. Thus, I give you love from my heart."*

*If there is some roughness between you and anyone, think the essence of these words as you give love:*

*"I have made a mistake in my thinking to allow you to seemingly hurt me. I recognize that you are merely doing what I invited, and that in reality neither you nor anyone else can hurt me. I am perfect now, always have been, and always will be. You can't change that. I now recognize that life is for giving love to you, so I now give you love from my heart."*

CHAPTER SEVEN

*Correcting Mass-Consciousness*

A couple of weeks ago Drew had his younger brother over for dinner. Will is twenty, a junior in college, and innocent in many ways. He knows of our relationship and is accepting so long as his friends don't find out. During dinner Will told us about a new boarder his mom and dad have. He concluded that he is gay because the way he swings his hips when he walks, because the way he sits on the sofa, and because his voice is slightly higher, among other such observations. Wanting to pamper Will, I found myself accepting without comment what he was saying.

After a few minutes I finally interrupted. "Wait a minute. We can't know he's gay because of these observations. It's all right if he is, but these are just misconceptions. The way a person walks or talks doesn't tell us what he wants to do with his body, or about his emotions."

I then told Will about the leather bars I've been to, the truck drivers I've known, and the urban-cowboys. He was all ears, and I realized he really had very little idea about who gay men and lesbians are.

I also realized how I have contributed over the years to this misunderstanding. I wish I had a dollar for every queer joke I've laughed at to preserve my cover. I'm ashamed to say I probably even added to the humor.

Even now I'm not immune to coddling some of these common misconceptions. Last Saturday Drew and I drove to Charlotte to see his older brother and sister-in-law. A mutual friend came up in conversation. "Think he's gay?" his sister-in-law asked. "He seems like it, doesn't he," I answered.

Seems like it!! I had fallen into the same damn trap. I had picked up on mass-consciousness and used that yardstick to judge our friend, just a few days after calling Will on the same error.

Now, I'm not being harsh on myself for doing that, only making a poignant observation. We can't help but have erroneous thoughts about gay men and lesbians, even though we know the stereotypes are simply not true. We can't help it because we are bathing in mass-consciousness.

We are aware of the vast sea of thoughts that all humanity shares. This sea is the sum total of all that humankind thinks. Since we're all connected, that reservoir of ideas flashes through us constantly. We can not turn them off. It's impossible to be unaware of them. We can't help but hear what the mass-mind thinks about homosexuality.

However, we gay men, lesbians, and enlightened heterosexuals can decide not to buy into it. Furthermore, we can also decide to correct the thinking for ourselves. Our decision not to buy into false beliefs and to correct our own thinking is paramount as spiritual initiates. Perhaps in this lies our greatest contribution to change world attitudes and world thoughts.

This theme keeps reappearing, but I'll say it again: We have the power within ourselves to change the prejudice and attacks because we have the power of our thoughts.

The power of thought is two-fold. First, as a group we can think Truth together many times more powerfully than thinking it alone. And second, an ounce of Truth corrects tons of untruth. This is simply the nature of Truth, as nature strives to regain balance.

We've already learned an example of the group power when we think *The Love Meltdown* together. Perhaps you've experienced it by now. We can do the same with any other thought that needs correcting. There are hundreds of thousands of groups in this country, many just for homosexuals and their supporters. One function of these groups must be to correct thoughts.

Let me remind you what potential lies in a group. The power of a group thinking a single Truth together under one roof is found by squaring the number of people. Only fifteen people thinking Truth together would have the power of 225 thinking Truth alone. Sixteen is the same as 256, to show what happens with even one more.

Our next spirexual experience, *The Mass-Consciousness Correction*, is for groups, and like all the other experiences, it is simple. Come up with about five Truths that you want to infuse into the mass-mind. Don't be concerned about the misconceptions your Truth needs to correct. We don't have to address them at all. Just dwell on the Truth. You can use the same Truths at each meeting, or you can compile a different list each time. If by chance an untruth creeps onto a list, don't worry. The tremendous power of groups is really only effective for Truth. False notions don't have the support of the cosmos and require far more people to have any effect.

A list of Truths might look like this:

*1. Everyone in all races is created with all of God's qualities.*

*2. Forgiveness is accomplished by giving love.*

*3. When humankind assaults nature with pollution, we are assaulting our own Self.*

*4. We are made in the image of God and already have all of God's qualities as our own without evolving.*

*5. Gay, lesbian, and non-gay sex are all divinely holy.*

When the list is agreed upon, the leader tells everyone to close the eyes and become centered and relaxed. Soft harmonic music is optional. After a minute or so, the leader speaks out the first Truth and tells the group to think it once. After thirty seconds of silence, the leader then tells them to think that same Truth a second time, followed by another thirty seconds of silence. Each of the Truths on the list is thought in this manner: two impulses, each followed by thirty seconds of silence.

We are part of humanity. We add to the sum total of mass-consciousness. This isn't a role we can accept or reject. If we want to keep buying into erroneous stereotyped thinking, that is what we'll be reinforcing. If we want to change it, we can. We are a significant bloc in that mass-consciousness. There is no excuse for it to be so full of misinformation. We have the power to refill that mass-consciousness with Truth.

All of us would like to be broad minded and accept other people's ideas. That's all fine, but the fact is that there are mountains of false beliefs about us. They are indeed false—unequivocally false, and they are interfering with our lives.

Truth is not a variable. It just is. We don't need to feel pompous to know it because it is available for everyone. Furthermore, we don't ever have to guess what is Truth. We can easily learn it by tapping the all-knowing intelligence of our Higher Selves, and we will learn how to do that in the next chapter. The answers from that source are Truth.

Truths are statements about love, the unified field. Truths express the order of creation. They are, therefore, at the fundamental fiber of nature. The mere utterance of such a basic concept sends thrills throughout all of creation, especially that sea of mass-consciousness. When the vibration of Truth echoes in mass-consciousness, it does so with such fury as to shatter anything out of tune with it—like the singer's high C shatters a goblet.

Untruth does not have this shattering ability. It's like the bass note that leaves only a small imprint. The shrill of Truth shatters.

Even one of us thinking Truth regularly shatters, to some degree, the untruth of mass-consciousness. Don't underestimate your own power of thinking alone. It is tremendous because of the nature of Truth. Thinking in a group is like exploding a hydrogen bomb, and thinking alone is like exploding an atomic bomb.

This is why our thoughts are so very important at this time in history. We are rearranging mass-consciousness. We must be aware constantly of what we think. This can't be over-emphasized.

Every place we turn we are reminded that we create what we think. I've alluded to this several times. Books have been written on it. Psychologists and physicians can relate thoughts to our health and sense of well-being. Thoughts not only influence how we view the world, but they actually attract what comes into our lives.

Everyone appears to have huge antennas forty feet tall scanning the airwaves. These are both transmitters and receivers. By our thoughts we send out messages of what we expect, believe, want, fear, or long for. Other people pick these up, and if they jibe with their own expectations, beliefs, desires, fears, or longings, they come to us to "help out." It's all perfect. Everyone is helping everyone else get what they broadcast they want.

Thoughts aren't private. All of creation is listening and anxious to help our thoughts come true. Our creation does begin with our thoughts. Quite literally, Mother/Father God's thought created the world. In the image of God, we are creators, and we create with thoughts also.

If we find ourselves thinking something inappropriate or something we don't want to experience, it's very easy to erase. We just say to ourselves, "That not correct. I cancel that." And it is done. We all have fear thoughts, or anger, or other inappropriate ideas that can be the foundation for our world tomorrow. We have them because they are floating around in mass-consciousness. When they come up, we can simply take note, disclaim them, and correct our thinking.

I've heard that God can't bear to say "no." Whatever we ask for, we get—even if we think we're joking. God will say "yes" without judgment to everything we think. All of the forces of nature come to manifest our expressed desires.

As enlightened leaders, it is our duty to monitor our thinking. We have the incentive because we know we are planting the seeds for tomorrow in our personal lives, and we are planting the seeds for how the world accepts lesbians and gay men. One reason we are here is to help clean away all the garbage in the sea of human consciousness. Maybe, just maybe, that is the only significant reason many of us are here.

## MASS-CONSCIOUSNESS CORRECTION
### *Affirming Truth To Cancel Error Belief*

*Compile a list of five affirmative Truths for a group to think together at the same time under one roof. The group is then lead through this meditation-like experience.*

*LEADER: "Close your eyes and get centered and relaxed."*
*(allow 1 minute)*
*LEADER: "Now think once: (read the first Truth from the list)."*
*(30 seconds of silence)*
*LEADER: "Now think once again: (read the first Truth from the list again)."*
*(30 seconds of silence)*
*Continue in this manner for about five separate affirmative Truths.*

CHAPTER EIGHT

## Channeling Your Higher Self

This chapter is like the recipe for chocolate fudge chiffon cake. The proof is in the eating. Like the cake recipe these words by themselves are quite bland without the experience they can give. We now expand *The Conscious Connection* to use it as an indispensable tool for learning Truth. We can even use it for guidance in our daily lives.

If you have sat quietly several times with the intention to notice your Higher Self signal, but it wasn't obvious, now is the time to take charge. Your Higher Self signal is not thrust upon you. You can decide what you want. If you don't like a particular signal, or if it hurts, or if you think other people might think you're spastic, or if it just doesn't come, then you can take charge.

Taking charge means you decide what the signal is to be, you practice it, then you expect to experience that signal during *The Conscious Connection*.

An easy Higher Self signal is the head rocking back and forth. Sit erect so your head pivots easily on the neck. Rock it back and forth to get the feeling. During *The Conscious Connection* get completely relaxed and ask for your Higher Self signal. Expect your head to rock back and forth. After a couple of minutes if it doesn't move, then take charge. Move it exactly like you practiced.

Once it starts moving, it will continue on its own. Allow *The Conscious Connection* to continue for at least ten more minutes. Keep your attention on the signal. If your mind wanders, just allow your attention to come back to the signal.

Practice being with your Higher Self signal every day for at least a week before adding the new experiences in this chapter. You have all the time you need, so develop these tools slowly.

In the same way you can take charge to get your Higher Self signal, you will take charge to get *Yes* and *No* signals. The *Yes* and *No* signals are used to get simple yes and no answers to questions. Like the Higher Self signal, they are some physical movement, sensation, vision, or feeling that you can notice when you ask a question during *The Conscious Connection.*

You can ask for the signals to come, or you can develop them. Let me tell you about mine. My *Yes* signal is a rotation of the head to the left three times. I start by sitting comfortably with my head and spine very vertical. My head is able to pivot on the neck, then the head rotates three times to the left. If you would like to develop that signal, practice until you feel quite comfortable with the movement.

My *No* signal is practically the same, except the head rotates only once. It moves more slowly than my *Yes* signal.

To get your *Yes* and *No* signals, go into *The Conscious Connection* and be with your Higher Self signal for about ten minutes. Then ask your Higher Self to give you a *Yes* signal. Expect the three rotation movements if that's what you practiced. If you decided to be open, expect something. It will come. Practice what comes a

58

few times, and then ask for your *No* signal. Expect the one rotation if that's what you want, or be open to another. It will also come.

Practice your *Yes* and the *No* signals for a few more minutes. Mix them up. Get quite comfortable with the movement, sensation, vision, or feeling, but don't use them to ask questions at this point. You must feel they are foolproof and reliable. This will take some practice, especially to break through your own doubts about all this. Practice is very important. Incorporate it into your daily—twice daily if possible—twenty minute experience of *The Conscious Connection.*

After a week or so being comfortable with all your signals every day, move on to the next spirexual experience, *Channeling Your Higher Self.*

In this experience you actually receive Truth and answers from your Higher Self—that *whole you* that is all-knowing intelligence. This procedure is similar to *The Conscious Connection,* except that once you have your signals down pat, you can eliminate the connected breathing if you want to. There are seven easy steps for this experience.

First, sit comfortably with your eyes closed and focus on the love pulsating from your heart to all of creation.

Second, think of some of God's qualities and unify with the natural forces of creation by claiming these same qualities as your own.

Third, allow your Higher Self signal to appear and keep it with you at all times, except when it is interrupted for the *Yes* and *No* signals.

Fourth, ask your Higher Self to feed you "thoughts of Truth that are appropriate at this time."

Fifth, listen. Listen to your thoughts along with the Higher Self signal.

Sixth, quietly speak out the thoughts given to you by your Higher Self. Periodically ask, "Is what I am saying correct?" Use your *Yes* and *No* signals for your answer. If the answer is no, find out where you made a mistake.

Seventh, when you are finished, keep your eyes closed for another two minutes. This is very important. If you come out too fast, you might feel irritable or rough for a short time.

In the early stages of channeling your Higher Self, only general statements of Truth will come to you. This will help you to locate those thoughts, because in the background you may continue to hear the static of an active mind that doesn't want to be left out.

A good example of this type of channeling is this book. Each day I secluded myself in a quiet place, got centered, then channeled my Higher Self and the Masters—more on *Channeling Our Masters* in Chapter Sixteen. In a real sense, this is *co-creating*. The basic ideas, experiences, and concepts came to me as I wrote. I had to put these into readable English on paper. I even embellished and added for clarity and transition. Of course, the stories are from my own life. It would have been most difficult to receive this knowledge without my own experiences, training, and memories.

In that way, this type of channeling, and indeed this book, is a fusion of Truth and everyday experiences. There is no doubt in my mind that you will be able to zero in on some aspect of universal knowledge, develop a clear understanding, then also channel a book to further mankind's awakening.

Practice this procedure daily from now on. However, only when you feel quite comfortable with it for several weeks should you start to ask specific questions. The answers can be narrated, or they can be answered with your *Yes* and *No* signals.

Ask if it is in your *"highest and wisest interest"* to ask the question about so and so. If not, find out why. It could be you already know the answer, or you need to work through the problem on your own without additional information. Finding out *Why not?* can be quite valuable knowledge in itself.

Frame your questions carefully because the words are taken literally, like a computer would. Avoid double meanings. State the whole question with nothing inferred.

When asking questions, use the words *"highest and wisest interest"* whenever possible. Those words truly do express your intention in everything you do, don't they? For instance, "Is it in my highest and wisest interest to move in with Elizabeth?"

Always ask the opposite. It can be in your highest and wisest interest to move in with Elizabeth and also not to move in with Elizabeth. You always have many options, and channeling can not tell you which choice to make among the many perfect ones. You must continue to exercise your free will and judgment. That's what makes living on earth like a fun game.

*Channeling Your Higher Self* is an invaluable tool, but only for receiving knowledge that is relevant for you to think at the present time.

This is very important to grasp: the channeling will tell you only what is wise for you to *think*—and that is what to think *for the present time.*

Our reality, our life, our experiences are what we think. When we figure out what to think, all aspects of our lives automatically fall into place. Furthermore, we can only think in the present. That's obvious. You can't think future or past, any more than you can jump from an airplane at any place or time where you are not.

Yet, often we dwell on what we did or are going to do. When that happens, we are missing what we are doing now.

God is everywhere present, not everywhere future or everywhere past. When we channel, we are unified with forces we identify as God—that is, all of nature, all of creation. That is only present.

It is usually senseless to ask questions dealing with what you should have thought yesterday. The same is true of tomorrow. You can not and will not receive any knowledge on what to do or think in the future, only the present.

I have struggled and struggled to learn the value of thinking for the present. Questions about lovers were my real teachers. In looking for that perfect love, I wanted to know who my life mate would be and when he would happen. Sound familiar? That answer was never available, but guidance for my present thinking always was.

I learned that Jack, Bill, and Andrew were men whom I could think of as perfect lovers. At the same time I learned not to think of Mark, Michael, and Frank in that category. Two days later I learned to stop thinking of pursuing Bill, but to add Greg to the list. At no time did I know how the future would turn out, but my focus for the moment was perfect.

This is the only way it can be. Another person has free-will, and you can't control that. And you have free-will. It is all a matter of many perfect choices you freely will, and they begin with your thoughts.

Well begun is half done. Thinking is the beginning of all of our experiences. Think the perfect thoughts now, and the future will be perfect, regardless of which options you choose.

It is very important you understand that this technique is a tool for *thinking in the present.* Your options will be expanded and your life will become much more dynamic and exciting.

*Channeling Your Higher Self* will take lots of practice before you are completely comfortable. Everyone can do it—indeed we have always channeled our Higher Selves, but we usually didn't listen. These tools simply give you a conscious connection so you can learn to rely on the input you're already getting. Take your time and let this experience unfold in an easy way. It is a major, major part of your spirituality.

## *CHANNELING YOUR HIGHER SELF*
### *Receiving Truth And Practical Guidance*

*A prerequisite for this experience is that you feel comfortable with your Higher Self signal and the Yes and No signals.*

*The seven steps in channeling your Higher Self are:*

*1. Sit comfortably with your eyes closed and focus on the love pulsating from your heart to all of creation.*

*2. Think of some of God's qualities and unify with the natural forces of creation by claiming these qualities as your own.*

*3. Allow your Higher Self signal to appear, and keep it with you at all times, except when it is interrupted for your Yes and No signals.*

*4. Ask your Higher Self to feed you Truth or an answer to a question that is appropriate for you at this time.*

*5. Listen to your thoughts along with your Higher Self signal, and speak out the Truth given to you in your thoughts by your Higher Self.*

*6. Using your Yes and No signals, periodically ask, "Is what I am saying correct?" If not, find out where you made a mistake.*

*7. Keep your eyes closed for two minutes afterward. Not to do so may cause irritability and roughness for a short time.*

*The guidelines for asking questions are:*

1. *Before asking any question, ask if it is in your "highest and wisest interest" to ask the question.*
2. *Frame your question carefully to avoid double meaning.*
3. *Always use the words "highest and wisest interest" in framing your question.*
4. *Always get an answer for the opposite, because you may be getting guidance that a wide range of choices are in your highest and wisest interest.*
5. *Ask only questions that are relevant for the present time. Do not ask about the past, the future, or predictions.*

# CHAPTER NINE

## *The Relationship Reality*

We now expand the concept of *Channeling Your Higher Self* to embrace an area few people have even thought about. It is a natural extension, but a type of channeling that is new to me. At least, I hadn't fully realized its potential. I have used this tool on many occasions now, but oddly enough, it came to me while writing the first draft of this book.

I drove with Drew to Bakersville, North Carolina for a gathering of gay men. We missed the weekend crowd of about sixty, since Drew had a final examination. Instead we arrived at the rustic ranch called Running Water near the summit of Rhone Mountain, only to find a dozen or so people.

My first inclination was to head right back to Chapel Hill, but we had come with a friend who more quickly picked up on the positive vibes. Lightning—and that's his real name—had gone to the same gathering ten years earlier with negative experiences, and he had come specifically to heal that. Since Drew and I adored Lightning, we decided to wait until morning to decide about leaving.

As we were introduced to people, it was all I could do to keep from snicking. Most had adopted fairy style names: Pine Cone, Heart Singer, Laughing Dragon, Crazy Owl, Pouhka, and River. For some reason, though, our friend Lightning still seemed to have a normal name.

Drew and I had long before decided we would have an open arrangement. To us that meant we could fondle and enjoy anyone safely without insertion. Little did I realize we had set ourselves up for a major reexamination. Two new additions to the group gave special intrigue and made us decide we ought to stay: Adam from Philadelphia—a twenty six year old collegiate style hockey player, and David from New York—a cute medical student.

Over the next couple of days, Drew and I became quite chummy and heartfelt with everyone. Drew especially demonstrated his love easily, and wallowed in expressing his affection. His cuddling and attention with the other guys didn't bother me at all, because I was just as much in heaven. The men with the strange names quickly became our long lost deep friends. We were indeed glad we had come.

On the third afternoon I wandered through the woods alone and stumbled onto Drew and Larry. They were splashing in the creek and home-made waterfall. Their nudity, sexual arousal, and unabashed affection somehow shook me, but I quickly contained my feelings. After all, these were the rules, and I thought I needed the liberality as much as Drew. Nevertheless, something inside was trying to be heard.

The next day I drove David to the top of the mountain for a hike on the Appalachian Trail. He ran far ahead, and I eventually stopped to meditate. We did have time, however, to express interests in each other, and he said he'd enjoy a three-way with me and Drew, a first for David.

When we got back I told Drew, who was delighted to hear David found him interesting. Within the hour, Drew and David retreated to a secluded bunk for adolescent making-out and nude frolicking. When I learned about that I felt a strong feeling of—of—well, I'm not sure. At the time, it struck me and everyone else as possessiveness or insecurity. Yet, it seemed like a greater voice yelling that we needed to reexamine our values, rules, and priorities.

David was cute, so I easily decided again to squelch the feelings and go along with the three-way Drew had arranged. That night David arrived at our tent. As soon as he crawled in, the feelings returned, and I felt worse than I've felt since I broke up with my last lover. Drew put his hand on me, and I abruptly moved it away. My emotions were out in the open, and I found myself saying to him, "This isn't right. If that's what you want, we won't last. I'll just leave. I know it."

I turned to a confused and bewildered David and told him to leave, that Drew and I needed to talk.

And talk we did. For two hours!! Everyone around must have been kept awake that night. We accused, argued, and occasionally kissed, only to get angry again. Suddenly, out of the blue, Drew said, "There's only one solution. We'll be totally, one hundred percent, monogamous."

As soon as he said it, I thought, "No, I can't commit to that, I'm sure."

At the same time a calmness came over me. The fears, anxieties, and horrible argumentative stance vanished. It was like a demon entity had suddenly left my body, and I sat up to take notice. I looked at Drew and said, "I don't know why, but those words seem to ring true. Let's go to sleep and look at this again in the morning."

The next day we left Running Water, but not before Drew managed to announce to everyone that we were now monogamous. Somehow I felt embarrassed, like my own insecurities and immaturity had created a fuss everyone knew about. It did indeed seem that way, except I couldn't help remember the sudden return to peaceful emotions when Drew spoke of monogamy the night before.

When we got home, I asked Drew to channel our Higher Selves with me so we could become clear on monogamy. He already felt it was correct, but I had my doubts.

The channeling was quite clear: it is in our highest and wisest interest to be monogamous. That does not mean, however, that monogamy is a general spiritual practice for everyone.

More important than answers about monogamy, we learned something mind-boggling about *relationships*: it is a type of entity in itself. It was our *relationship* that was nudging us into monogamy, at first gently, then harder and harder. Our *relationship* was doing that. When Drew voiced the solution that night in the tent, I felt the clear presence of the *relationship*. It turned from discomfort to peace, as fast as blinking my eyes.

We learned that *relationship* between any two people is actually an energy. It matters not if it's between two men, two women, or a man and a woman. It matters not their sexual involvement. The phenomenon is the same. All the gross and subtle energies of one person are combined with those of the other. The sum total is the *relationship*. The energies are not added together, so as to augment and cancel each other like sound, electricity, or light. Instead, all the energies of the two people are present in this new bundle of energy. It actually does exist, and when science becomes more sophisticated, the *relationship* will be located and measured.

Furthermore this new bundle of energy, the *relationship*, has intelligence and consciousness. As long as Drew and I am together, we can be guided by the intelligence of our *relationship*. That is what was happening when we felt the need to be monogamous. We had been interfering with our best interests by pursuing outside sex partners. That was cutting into our fun together and into our overall goals. So, our *relationship* acted. It spoke loudly in our thoughts and emotions. The issue was ultimately one of survival for the *relationship*, and the message was bound to get through. For other couples, their *relationships* could very well have a totally different message on monogamy. Or, for me in a *relationship* with someone else, the message could be different. The message might even be different next year with Drew, since nothing is static, but ever-changing. Remember, we can only be certain of what is best for our thoughts for the present time.

It is really impossible for me alone to know what is best for the *relationship*. I can't know that because I don't know Drew's energies and needs, nor how they mesh with mine. That's why in the scheme of nature a whole separate, intelligent, and conscious energy is born when two people come together. We are intimately connected to that new energy, and it can be a guiding light if we open ourselves to it.

I've been speaking in terms of lover *relationships*, but the phenomena doesn't end there. Every conceivable type and size of *relationship* has this energy and consciousness: you and your mother, you and your separate friends, you and your sister, your whole family, your whole household, your class at school, your support group, your city, your race group, your countrymen, everyone on earth.

We've discussed mass-consciousness. That's what this is. Mass-consciousness is really an energy made up of all the people in a group. That consciousness contains all the knowledge about everyone in that group. It holds their ideas and aspirations, and it contains all their beliefs. It also knows Truth, and it can nudge and guide the group. What we experience with a lover, we also experience as a nation. There is a *relationship*—a mass-consciousness—for each and every conceivable combination. The immensity of the *relationship* energies is staggering, but nature is infinite, and there are no boundaries. There's plenty of room for all these combinations.

When Drew and I realized our *relationship* was more than me and him, but an actual energy, it was very exciting. It made sense that we could say "our *relationship* needs...," or "our *relationship* is...," or "it's in the highest and wisest interest of our *relationship* that...."

At Running Water, our friend Lightning started a *relationship* with Adam, the collegiate hockey player. So far, it has survived beyond the gathering, and Adam has moved to Chapel Hill. As I observe their new *relationship*, I can see clearly these basic principles. Before his move, I checked their compatibility with astrology for my

71

own curiosity. There are many ways to do this, as you know if you've studied astrology. I simply checked to see how the planets on one of their charts made aspects to the other's planets. As I did this, it dawned on me that the combination is the fingerprint of the new *relationship*. When two or more people come together, each brings all of his or her traits, talents, strengths, and weaknesses. These combine for a totally new and unique entity. There are new energies to create, new energies to enliven spirituality, and new energies to set up a household. There are combinations for love, for sex, and for intellectual discussions. The *relationship* can also be lacking in these, but stronger in many others. Each *relationship* brings forth energies that are the sum total of each person in it.

This was really a profound break-through for me in understanding my *relationship* with Drew. Our *relationship* has life, has energy, has intelligence, and has consciousness. Our *relationship* knows what is best for it and for each of us.

It's like my Higher Self," I thought, "except it's a Higher Self for the two of us. I wonder if I can channel it, like I can channel my Higher Self? Mmmm. I wonder."

I decided to find out. I sat up, got centered, received my Higher Self signal, and asked if I could also channel Drew's and my *relationship*. "Yes" was the clear answer, so I asked for the *relationship* signal. It was a flow of energy pulsating into my head and out my mouth.

I first asked just to feel the *relationship*. A distinct emotional shift took place, and I could feel the state of the *relationship*. It was the feeling of peace and love and security. I also knew the anguish I felt in the tent at Running Water was a feeling of the *relationship* at that time. When we finally understood its message on monogamy, we both experienced a shift in its state that night. What discovery! We can actually monitor the state of our *relationships*, and we can actually feel them!

I asked questions using my *Yes* and *No* signals. "Is it in Drew's and my best interest to be monogamous at this time?" Yes. "Is the *relationship* guiding us into being monogamous?" Yes. "Did the *relationship* feed me the feelings and emotions at Running Water to bring the issue of monogamy to a head?" Yes.

Drew and I have been thinking about moving to Maui, and we have channeled from our Higher Selves that it is a wise move. So I asked, "Is the *relationship* guiding us to move to Maui at this time?" Yes. I also verified that the move is a *relationship* move. That is, if we were not together such a move might not be in our individual highest and wisest interest. Or it might be for only one of us.

*The Relationship Connection* as a spirexual experience is quite easy when you've mastered the techniques up to this point. The procedure is the same as *Channeling Your Higher Self.* Get a specific *relationship* signal that you can use for any *relationship*. You don't need a separate signal for the *relationship* with your lover, another for your mother, another for your boss, etc. Once you have the *relationship* signal, you hone in on whichever *relationship* you want. It's that simple.

Using this tool we can quickly learn all about our various *relationships.* Furthermore, we can empower whichever ones we want by our mere intention. That's important to understand. We are not victims or slaves to these energy fields called *relationships*. We decide which ones are to be dominant. The decision doesn't even need to be conscious. It's a matter of focus or intention. Knowing they exist and that we can empower them is the first step in gaining greater control over our lives. We are still in control, but we do live with and amongst other people. We must also choose which of these *relationships* we will empower. By our desire and intention, Drew and I empowered our *relationship* with each other. Consequently, it did and could make its needs known, in this instance on the issue of monogamy.

You can monitor any *relationship*, but for it to be really empowered requires the desire and intention of each member, even if implied.

By carefully monitoring our principle *relationships*, we can improve their quality. This experience makes the monitoring quite easy and fun with time and practice.

Drew and I came back early from Running Water so we could join the Gay Pride March in Raleigh. Thousands of men and women from all over North Carolina marched to the State Capitol for a rally that included two open-minded, enlightened non-gay politicians advocating "Gay Rights Now." During the march and the rally, I really felt like I belonged to these people. I could feel our group *relationship*, but it was months later that I truly appreciated what that *relationship* is. Perhaps you're having similar revelations as you read this.

We do have a distinct *relationship* with gay men, lesbians, and non-gay supporters. For most homosexuals this is a primary *relationship* that can't be ignored or denied. It is indeed a special energy with intelligence, purpose, and consciousness.

All along the parade route we yelled, "What do you want? Gay Rights! When do you want it? Now!"

This yell echoes throughout America in these Gay Pride Marches. It is extremely powerful and illustrates the potency of group thoughts. By marching and by yelling, we are empowering that consciousness to muster all the forces in nature and to guide each of us so the goal is quickly realized.

I'm sorry I missed the march on Washington, but I felt it because I am part of the *relationship.* It is very important that we nourish every opportunity to empower it: marches, rallies, parties, fund-raisers, political campaigns, or whatever. Some of us are inclined to be more activists than others, but all gay men and lesbians are all part of the group.

To be spiritual is to recognize our many *relationships* and to empower the ones we want. No longer do we need to wonder how any of our *relationships* are doing. We can easily find out. Furthermore, we can know precisely how to make them more fulfilling and successful for everyone.

*THE RELATIONSHIP CONNECTION*
*Channeling The Highest Good*
*For Your Relationships*

*Use the same procedures and guidelines for Channeling Your Higher Self. Ask for and get a relationship signal, then state the relationship you wish to connect with. You can feel the present state of the relationship, and you can channel relevant knowledge about the relationship.*

CHAPTER TEN

## *The Soul Site*

Mentally locate the spot in the back of your head, about an inch inside your skull and directly behind your eyes. When you have located that spot and felt it for a few moments, let your attention be with an imaginary string from that spot down your spine. Now, before reading further, close your eyes and experience this spot and string.

Did you notice a calmness there? With the attention on that region, could you feel a sense of well being? Did you get a feeling of immortality?

This is obviously a key point in our physiology, but if you think I am now going to tell you that region is the site of your soul, your Higher Self, think again. To isolate a single spot or line and to say that is where the soul is would be too limiting for the Self.

For us to understand the site of the soul we need to go back to one of our very first premises: we are made in the image of God, and God is everywhere present. There is no place where God is not. God is in everything, and is even beyond everything. In a very real sense the universe is God's physical body. Just as we know we are more than our physical bodies, so is God more than the universe.

Since God is omnipresent, how then can we possibly say we are made in the image of god? After all, we have only a human shell for our physical body, while God has the universe for His. Well, therein lies one of our grand illusions. We are not what we appear to be.

Humankind is finally beginning to recognize the illusion. For instance, everywhere we go we carry with us auras of energy extending many feet in all directions. Some auras have been seen to extend for miles. These energy fields display our emotions, our physical health, our attitudes, and our divinity. Cameras can now photograph them. Instruments can read the energy. No longer are these auras just figments in the imagination of cultists.

Thus, although we do inhabit our bodies, we are clearly more. The energy auras around us are just small hints of our true beings, our souls, our Higher Selves. Those auras are still physical parts of us. Beyond and within we continue to exist, and spread, and permeate, and manifest. We are literally omnipresent. Just like our Creator, we are everywhere present, reaching beyond the far reaches of the universe. That is the site of our souls—all of creation.

There is nowhere we do not exist. The distant galaxies are just as much us as are our little fingers here on earth. God shares His/Her body with us, so the universe is also our body. Yet, like God, we are even more than that. Incomprehensible? Perhaps, but only because we have buried our attention in an illusion that we are here, and now, and this, and nothing else.

Here, and now, and this? Yes. But much, much more. So much more that we have no boundaries, no limits, and no handicaps, except those we have imposed by our thoughts.

For some reason we have chosen to focus on the earth, our bodies, and this time frame, which is fine and the way it should be. However, we then assume that is all we have. It is most difficult to comprehend we are the universe. The greatest scientists are both lights years away from realizing this and yet appear to be on the verge of proving it.

In Chapter 5 we touched briefly on Einstein's General Relativity, his Special Relativity, and his Unified Field Theory. He showed that space and time are really the same thing. He also showed that matter and energy are the same. He died before he could show that gravity—that force that holds all of creation's physical bodies together—is also the same as space, time, energy, and matter. Oddly enough, Einstein's discoveries throw remarkable insight into our own *soul-site.*

We agree we are on earth. We agree we are in the twentieth century. We agree we are matter. We agree we are also energy. But, wait. In reality these are all the same. Of course, we don't experience them as the same. That is the grand illusion. There is in Truth no boundary between matter and space. Our physical matter is the same as energy. It is the same as electricity, as light, as ultraviolet rays, as sound, and so on. It then melts into space and time.

This is so simple, yet it completely destroys our orientation. Even those people who believe in immortality hold the notion we exist as an entity that floats from here to there down through the ages. In fact, we exist everywhere all at once, at the same time, and for all time, which is happening at a single moment!!

So, that's where your soul is: in the midst of creation and intricately woven into it. We're not a part of it. We are it, because the universe does not have parts at its most refined level. This universe is God's body, and He/She is yet more than that. This universe is my body, and I am yet more than that. This universe is your body, and you are yet more than that. This universe is the body of all of us at once, and we all are yet more than that.

This is why we can say we are all one. This is why we are all connected. All of us are all space, all time, all matter, all energy, and all gravity. Each of our souls resides in all of that at once.

However, that's not our experience today, is it? It is not what we see, hear, taste, smell, and feel daily. How does it all mesh?

We have the ability, as souls created in God's image, to focus on any aspect of our Selves. It isn't important now to know precisely why we chose to focus on earth in the twentieth century, just that we did. Creation in its absolute Oneness would be boring. To wallow in timelessness or spacelessness, or abstract energy, or unmanifest matter would be uneventful, to say the least. We crave fun, play, and variety. That's what we have here on earth—and on many other wonderful playgrounds, I might add.

Around us is the constant play and display of all the forces of nature. It's fun. It's so much fun that we seem to have gotten completely enraptured with it. Like a child at the carnival, we're often overshadowed by the images around us. We sometimes think they are *it*, when they are only a display of *it*.

Since we share creation as the site of our souls, it's like we all live in the same house. What is mine is yours, and what is theirs is ours, and everything is really you. Even the leaf on the tree is you. And me. You and I are one with the leaf because it is also a display of that basic oneness.

Since this is true, why did I begin this chapter by drawing your attention to the spot behind your eyes? There is something about our nervous systems and our physiology in that region that brings us the experience of our true nature.

After all, we do have a human body. It is a display of creative intelligence. Within that display we have stored all the knowledge of who and what we are. By simply focusing on that spot and the line down the spine, we seem to elicit some of that memory. For that reason, it is okay to consider this the site of your soul. It seems to hold the memory of your soul.

That initial exercise is our next spirexual experience, *The Soul Site*. Any time you want, let your attention be with that spot behind your eyes, and from there down your spine. You can do this when going to sleep, or when driving the car. Anytime is appropriate. The result is always a calmness and a reassurance that everything is fine. You won't know the details of your origin, but you will feel the permanence of your nature. You'll sense your oneness with creation, and you'll remember your God qualities.

If you're ever having problems about being a gay man or a lesbian, this is a particularly good exercise. It reestablishes your fundamental nature, which is at once gay, non-gay, male, and female. Being gay now in this life does not in the least bit change your basic nature, any more than being six feel tall changes it. Your being gay or lesbian is just another way to enjoy the diversity of nature. It's another display of your infinite Self. Although we often like to make a big thing of our choice in sexuality, it really is nothing more than that. In terms of energy, matter, space, time, and gravitation, it gets lost in the shuffle.

In fact, the real goal of gay movements is to show that being homosexual isn't particularly significant. That, of course, is the simple truth. All souls have the same site. We are all everything. We are all everywhere. All the confrontations on sexuality are really "much ado about nothing"—to steal some Shakespeare.

### THE SOUL SITE
#### Feeling Peace And Well-Being

*Mentally locate the spot behind your eyes and about an inch from the back of your skull. Keep your attention there, with your eyes open or closed. After a few moments expand your attention down the spine from that spot. This experience can be done at any time, and is particularly helpful to regain composure, calmness, and a sense of well-being.*

## CHAPTER ELEVEN

## *Bellowing Beauty*

I am grateful to my lovers for teaching me Truth. They each in their own way gave me pieces of the puzzle of life. Of course, that's the real underlying reason we mate up. Our closest ties unveil for us the hidden wonders of the universe.

I'm too close to Drew right now to see clearly his precise contribution. There are many, I'm sure, but one stands out already: his liberal use of the word *beautiful.*

A day has never dawned for me since I met him without the glorious words "Good morning, Beautiful." These words are not merely a habit, like my "Oh, really?" or "Know what I mean?" Drew actually does see such beauty around him that he must bellow it out.

To see the beauty around us is to see the beauty in our Selves. To feel our own beauty is to feel the beauty in others. To recognize our own beauty is to salute the beauty in all of creation.

Within us lies all the beauty of the cosmos. We are love. We are the unified field. We are matter, energy, time, space, and gravity. We are *That.* When we see our own beauty, and when we voice gratitude for it, we are paying homage to consciousness everywhere. Actually, we are worshiping God in the simplest and most meaningful way.

The DNA molecule in our genes carries all the information for our physical existence. It is like a computer that has recorded every bit of knowledge necessary to carry us from birth to death. It regulates our growth and matures us. It differentiates the organs, senses, and special body parts. It even links us to our species. Biologists marvel at the exactness of the DNA, and each new discovery about it unfolds another layer of its connection to life everywhere.

The *SOUL DNA* is the "master computer" that stores all information about creation so your body DNA can carry out its function. All information in the *SOUL DNA* is for your use. Of course, what it regulates is you in reality. With this linkage you can be any place with the speed of thought. You can connect with any other part of the cosmos with the speed of intention.

As farfetched as that may sound, each of us can and does do this, and we do it without interfering with anyone else doing the same thing. Most of us haven't done it since beginning this incarnation, though.

This is almost unfathomable. We are just too used to space and time constraints.

"If I'm here, you can't be here also" is a law of physics, and it is correct for the physical world, as far as it goes. However, time, space, and matter all melt into the same at this *SOUL DNA* level. There we share the same *SOUL DNA* and the same body of the universe with each other and God.

The *SOUL DNA* is infinite in its capacity, and that giant "master computer" can let each of us access any part of the cosmos, or Truth, or experience all at once. It is our unrestricted, unfettered link to each other and creation. That is our birthright.

Therefore, to see the beauty in another person is to see the beauty in your own Self. Even to see the beauty in a flower is see the beauty in your own Self. Both you and the flower are of the cosmos and hold the entire cosmos within its structure, just as a small chip of the hologram contains the entire hologram picture. The flower and your Self are both governed by the same *SOUL DNA*. Both are locked into space and time for here and now, but exist also in the infinite.

This is why seeing the beauty in another person is the same as seeing the same beauty in your Self. Another person is just another expression of that infinite *SOUL DNA*, which is the real you.

These concepts are both uplifting and baffling. They give us a good feeling, as does all Truth, yet they are as hard to grasp as a cloud. It is not important to figure this out intellectually—not the least bit important. In fact, the awareness we have of the cosmos or metaphysics is not gauged by how well we can write an essay on our infinite connection and the unified field. No. Many aware and enlightened people have never heard of these concepts.

The test is rather our perception of beauty. Do you look at a sunset and see beauty? Many people even deprive themselves of taking the time to look. Do you seek those glorious moments around you and marvel at nature's beauty? This is awareness.

Do you see the beauty of a cockroach? A mosquito? A house fly? To love their beauty does not mean we need to enjoy their annoyance, but seeing their beauty is awareness.

Last night a friend came over for dinner. She has recently fallen in love, so most of our conversation dwelled on her new girl friend. Drew asked "What do you like best about her?"

"She likes me. She really seems to like me," our friend answered.

When we fall in love, we are really falling in love with our Self. Someone has dared to see our beauty and to express it. Our response is the feeling of being in love. Of course. We are love. We are beauty. When we see that beauty, we are bound to feel love as a side effect. It's inevitable. Our friend did indeed feel love because she had her beauty verified.

What a gift it is for a loved one to tell us we're beautiful!! The very core of our nature is enlivened. We experience the soul level and our link to everyone. Then, quite naturally the next step is to actually feel our connection to our beloved.

"I feel as though we're never separated." Or, "I've never felt so complete." Or, "We seem to know what each other is thinking." Of course! This is the natural result of being in love, of feeling your own beauty, of being in tune with the infinite. Those phrases are three ways to say the same thing.

We all have people we love, yet how often do we tell someone he or she is beautiful? Too seldom. How often do we tell our friends they're beautiful? Hardly ever. How often do we tell strangers they're beautiful? Never.

If ever we could say "shame on us," it is for this, but shame is not a valid concept. We need not curse our neglect, or place blame, or be shamed. We simply need to turn on the light of beauty now.

Now! Right now, think of someone and say "You're beautiful." You know that at some level he or she can hear you. We've experienced that with *The Love Meltdown.*

You can't think "You're beautiful" too often. Think these words for people passing you on the street. Think them for the butterfly slowly flopping its wings on the long flight south. Think them for the stray dog. Think them for the flower blossom. Let every thought be laced with the beauty around you. You are, of course, merely praising your Self. Yet, without trying to intellectually understand that, you are fully aware of it. You feel it, and you reap the full benefit of knowing it. Besides, this is not something you need to learn. You already have the knowledge; it's built into the *SOUL DNA.*

If you have a lover, or live with someone, let "Good morning, beautiful" be the first words each day to him or her. Your relationship will bloom. Your day will prosper.

When I first started saying "You're beautiful," I must admit I was shy. I was even shy in saying it to Drew, who said it every morning without compunction. I'm not sure why bellowing beauty is so difficult for most of us. I suspect everyone notices some degree of reticence. With a little tenacity and practice, it will become second nature, and the joys of the experience will quickly overshadow that bashfulness.

"Beautiful" is a very powerful word, and it is my favorite. However, we can use lots of expressions and synonyms to say the same thing. "You have a special sparkle today." "Your eyes are shining." "You're stunning." "You're quite handsome, you know." "You're very pretty."

One of my favorite pastimes is to have a brief intimate contact with a stranger. By intimate, I don't mean sexual. People are always open to a sincere compliment that doesn't threaten their private space. At the checkout line in the supermarket, don't be afraid to tell the woman next to you her hairdo is gorgeous. Don't be afraid to notice a beautiful shirt, or any other article of clothing that was obviously carefully chosen. Whenever you approach someone, however, be certain the compliment is unconditional, quick, and non-invasive. If you compliment simply as the first step on the make, it looses its punch. That's not to say never be on the make. That's a natural part of life, but it dampens what I'm talking about: the unconditional recognition of someone's beauty.

This is *The Beautiful Beatitude*. In time this will be the outward hallmark of spiritual people. We will be extoling the beauty of everyone and everything around us. In doing so, we will be giving love to Mother/Father God, to Nature, to the Universe, and to our Selves. Above all, we will be enlivening our awareness.

We can't see beauty without broadening our awareness. Our vision is awakened in so many ways with this experience. As a man thinks, so he is. Think beauty, and your experience becomes beauty. Think beauty, and you radiate beauty for everyone. Think beauty, and your heart opens to touch the infinite. In your mind the infinite may remain a hazy abstraction, but in your heart, the infinite will paint the feelings of joy, and bliss, and happiness. This is our gift to ourselves by simply saying "You're beautiful" to someone.

### THE BEAUTIFUL BEATITUDE
*Voicing The Beauty You Are*

*Bellow beauty with these four new habits:*

*1. Say "Good morning, beautiful" to the first person you see each day.*
*2. Think "You're beautiful" for all life forms.*
*3. Think "You're beautiful" for strangers that pass by you.*
*4. Say the equivalent of "You're beautiful" with compliments to everyone as often as possible.*

*When you think or say "You're beautiful" or the equivalent, feel that you are affirming your own beauty because we are all one. Know also that your thoughts and words of beauty return to grace your own experiences.*

# CHAPTER TWELVE

## *Body Beautiful*

A woman I dated spent a great deal of energy and thought hating her body. She even cut off one of her toes because her large feet wouldn't accommodate the narrow shoe fashions!

One of my friends is quite stout. She fights hunger pains most of the day. A strict starvation diet is a way of life for her because she would rather be petite. Of course, the starvation inevitably leads to a binge, which creates more anger about her body. She has gone through scores of affirmations, mind treatments, hypnoses, and regressions, but her large boned frame simply won't shrink!

An old lover of mine has a sexy, slim swimmer's body with tight buns and great muscle tone. Is he satisfied? No. He goes to the weight room every other day, works up a heavy sweat pumping iron, then admires his bulk in the mirror. An hour later, his muscles deflate, like letting air out of a balloon. "I can't stand it," he would scream at me. "You work out fifteen minutes, and it stays built up. But look at me. Nothing."

These thoughts are not secret. They hit our bodies like a stick hits a drum. Each cell is bathed in the reverberating thought, "I hate you, I hate you."

What kind of work would you do for someone who constantly voiced dissatisfaction, hate, or disgust? Not quality, I'm sure.

Let's look at our wonderful machinery we call body in a slightly different way. It functions like a mini-universe. There are billions of cells. Each one is alive with consciousness. Think about this. Your body is not just you, but rather it is a collection of bodies for billions of other creatures that are conscious and aware.

Each cell relates to its universe, as we do to planet earth—or perhaps even as planet earth relates to the milky way. Each cell is specialized, and each cell has the intelligence needed to know how and what to do. It knows the nutrients, minerals, salts, electrolytes, water, or oxygen it needs, and then pulls them out of its environment. If the material isn't there, it improvises as best it can.

The cells are clustered together into organs and body parts, each with a particular function. Each of these parts also has consciousness, as indeed does all life. We humans are so egotistical that we often think that we have a monopoly on consciousness, awareness, and feelings. That's not the case. Our bodies are comprised of an entire creation of conscious beings, each with a purpose and a desire to serve. They range from the cell, to the individual organs, to the whole body. Each is a life form that exists in its own right.

We are not just our physical bodies. Temporarily we use it to anchor ourselves into the twentieth century on planet earth. We each have our own immutable permanent body of light that is the Self. However, the physical body we identify with is only our current ship of state.

91

Every being responds to its environment. We are no exception. When we're working for people who don't like us, we do sloppy work, give up, become depressed, or quit. It is the same with each cell. It does its work best when it is surrounded by praise and the feelings of love.

The "I hate you" thought does vibrate throughout the body. It is picked up, heard, and felt by every single cell and organ we so desperately need to enjoy life. Likewise, the "I love you" thought bathes them to produce an entirely different atmosphere.

We now recognize what difference a happy, loving home makes for a child. We know that appreciated workers increase productivity. Happiness and love at home and the work place surely must outrank a child's allowance or a worker's wage.

We have ignored those same principles for our beautiful body. Now is the time for everyone to turn this around with a special kind of spiritual experience, *Body Beautiful.* This is so simple it might seem a waste of energy.

*Body Beautiful* is simply relating to the physical body your feelings of love for it. Run your hands all over your body while saying "I love you," or "I am grateful to you," or "You're beautiful." The exact words are not important. You need only convey love and appreciation for the physical body you now inhabit.

One of my favorite ways to unify with my body is with *The Love Meltdown.* While running my hands all over my body, I say to it, "I give you my love, I give you my heart, I receive your love, I receive your heart." I know this practice has kept my middle aged body not only in perfect health, but looking and acting much younger.

Indeed, I do love my body, and I'm not bashful about telling anyone. We label it "polite" to praise someone else's body. We say we're "conceited" to praise our own. Nonsense! Praising and loving your body is no less than *good management.* You have billions of little beings working in your "factory." Be a good manager. Praise and love them privately. Praise and love them publicly. They do respond.

This does not mean we don't get rid of extra pounds, if indeed they are more than just a body type. We always do what we can from our side to have a gorgeous, healthy body. The point is we never stop loving it in the process. We actively send the love and gratitude it deserves.

As spiritual people, we need to do everything in our power to give our bodies maximum working conditions. Any good manager would do that. I won't go into detail, but here are some very basic points.

Exercise regularly. After all, you take your dog for a daily walk. Do the same for your body. Find the kind of routine both you and your body will enjoy. Then make a pact to exercise regularly.

Eat correctly. This is different for everyone, and seems to change periodically as well. There are common sense guidelines, however. Fresh food is preferred whenever possible. Try to avoid additives, even those added to the feed of beef or poultry. Neither starve yourself, nor overeat. Greasy, salty, sugary, junk foods are usually just that—junk.

Eliminate recreation drugs, whether eaten, smoked, or mainlined. Besides destroying cells, they cut right into our ability to experience such simple spiritual practices as *The Conscious Connection* and *Channeling Your Higher Self.*

Even tobacco is not for the spiritual person. Use alcohol sparingly, if at all.

Sleep at regular intervals and for the amount of time your body needs. During the day have periods of rest, including some form of meditation such as *The Conscious Connection.*

Every person's body is a unique creation. There are no hard and fast rules that can apply for everyone. Fortunately, we need not guess. We can ask our bodies what they need or want with our next spirexual experience, *The Body Bond.* We can literally locate and strengthen the conscious bond we already have with our bodies.

*The Body Bond* uses the same basic tools you learned in *Channeling Your Higher Self.* Get centered using *The Conscious Connection.* When you feel centered and your Higher Self signal is clearly present, say to your Higher Self, "I want to bond with my physical body. Give me a *Yes* signal when the bond is complete." After you get the *Yes* signal, you can channel your physical body just like you channel your Higher Self.

Using this method, I have become close friends with my body. We have total trust in each other, and like an effective marriage, we communicate openly.

I learned that my body enjoys ten minutes of sauna, but no more. It wants me to rest ten minutes after the sauna, though. Steam rooms are not its favorite, because sweating is easier in the sauna. Hot tubs are not at all to its liking. Now, that was news to me, since hot tubs are my first choice, and saunas my last. However, since changing the routine in the wet area at the YMCA, I do feel better.

I regularly channel my body—in the sauna, naturally—and we have a chat to see how things are going and if it needs something. I've also learned lots about the best foods for me and the kind of exercise my body needs.

Bonding regularly with my body and actively responding to its physical needs is the first step toward perfect health. That is the gift from a body that's loved and listened to.

### BODY BEAUTIFUL
#### *Giving Your Physical Body*
#### *Love and Gratitude*

*Run your hands all over your body while thinking and feeling love and gratitude for it with words such as "I love you," or "I am grateful to you," or "You're beautiful."*

### THE BODY BOND
#### *Channeling Your Physical Body*
#### *To Learn Its Needs*

*Get centered using The Conscious Connection. When your Higher Self signal is clearly present, say to your Higher Self, "I want to bond with my physical body. Give me a Yes signal when that bond is complete." After you get the Yes signal, you can channel your physical body just like you channel your Higher Self.*

CHAPTER THIRTEEN

## The Public Pat

Last weekend Drew and I went to a summer afternoon concert in the park. About fifty feet in front of our blanket were two women. They didn't stand out in the crowd, and I only noticed them when they left. They gathered their blanket and picnic basket. Just as they had everything under their arms and started walking away, one reached over to the other and gave a quick hug, like a half embrace. They glanced at each other, smiled, and walked out. I'm sure only a few people saw them, and I'm also sure they offended no one. Yet the wonderful vibrations they sent into the air must have forever improved public acceptance of homosexuals to some extent.

We complain we can't show public affection, yet we shiver at the thought. That fear has returned and returned to haunt us. We get exactly what we've put out into the atmosphere, and we wonder why we can't show public affection. As men and women think, so are they. Feel beauty around you, and it returns. Voice beauty, and it returns. Feel or voice fear, or dwell on the injustices, and they return.

Even our most enlightened heterosexual friends never think, "Oh, it's time we condoned public affection by two women or two men." That thought never occurs to them. That step is up to us. We're invisible and most non-gay people feel they know no homosexuals well, if at all. My mother once told me she only knew me and my lover, yet I know of several others she knows but hasn't identified.

People simply do not realize who we are, and it is up to us to introduce ourselves. We're like the black child being raised by two racial bigots who are blind. When the Truth is out, the love that binds all humanity will melt false beliefs about us.

That gentle tug, that squeeze of the hand, that wink, that smile, that pat on the back—these are all possible in public without offending anyone. These are signals of who we are, and we can reshape society with these signals. They are universal statements of Truth with emotion that we thrust with impelling force into the atmosphere. They not only return to us as powerful seeds of our next experiences, but they cleanse a great deal of untruth about us on their journey. These public pats are absolutely essential for gaining an open respectable place in society. We must feel comfortable with ourselves and our relationships. We can affirm that by an unobtrusive public gesture of affection.

Years ago it was accepted behavior in some communities to belittle Blacks. We denied them the right to eat in some restaurants, or drink from some water fountains, or sit in some seats, or swim in some pools, or live in some houses, or have some jobs, or go to some schools. The Blacks started to exert changes. A few dared to eat where forbidden. A few dared to apply for schools and jobs closed to them. A few dared to sit where denied. Gradually, the whole system started to fall. Now many of the most ardent supporters of integration are embarrassed by their own illogical position of thirty years ago. The positive attitudes and thoughts of the Blacks under an enlightened leadership that understood these principles brought results. Their thoughts, actions, and words returned to to them to begin removing slavery-de-facto.

In the same way, we must set our sights on what we want and then act. The unoffensive public gesture of love is the beginning, and it is important enough to be treated as a spiritual experience. Let's call it *The Public Pat.* It is not a full blown open mouth kiss. It isn't sexually explicit, or even implicit. It is only a simple love acknowledgement. More than likely, it will be unnoticed, but the emotion and Truth of love will give it power to rock creation, cleanse mass-consciousness, and return to us. We truly can change the world by clearing our fears to show love publicly.

You dear open-minded non-gays can really help by encouraging and praising our public affection. You can allow it in your homes, even in the presence of children. After all, there is nothing obscene about affection between any two people. The sooner a child can learn this, the faster will the curtain of prejudice fall. We need your help, encouragement, acceptance, and love. The first inroads into heterosexual acceptance of our love truly begins with you.

When Drew's sister married recently, she unwittingly gave us a public pat. It happened in the Duke University Gardens with a hundred or so wedding guests watching. The bride's immediate family gathered around her and the broom for pictures, while I wandered about fifty yards down the terraced walkway.

Drew's sister yelled, "Where's Roger? Roger! Come on up here. You're family." I cringed, gathered my composure, and walked briskly to join them. I knew that most of the guests and family members watching were learning about Drew and me for the first time. I knew his parents were embarrassed. And deep down inside, I was delighted.

A few weeks later Drew and I went to a picnic with his mother, father, younger brother, sister, and new brother-in-law. On the way we discussed the need for lesbians and gay men to begin showing public affection. The ideas felt good to him. After all, Drew is quite affectionate anyway and was a gay rights advocate to his family way back in high school. Public touching always seemed a part of Drew's normal reactions to people.

"Let's begin today," I suggested. "At some point in full view of your whole family, let's give each other a loving gesture."

"Fine," he answered, like it would be no challenge at all.

At one point about an hour into the picnic, I rested my hand on Drew's shoulder. He tensed slightly and found reason to stoke the coals on the hamburger grill. That was all we did the whole afternoon! Not once was Drew able to comfortably touch me, even though his sister and new husband cuddled arm in arm. Even his parents touched and patted affectionately.

"But Drew," I said on the way home, "you've always been physical with people. Hugging comes naturally for you."

"You're my lover," he answered, "and they know it. It's just different."

We experienced that *The Public Pat* is indeed not easy. Somehow though, I felt a sense of satisfaction for at least putting my hand on his shoulder. It gave me a tremendous feeling of freedom.

It would not be long, however, before I would experience again how difficult it is to show public affection. I drove Lightning and Adam to the airport. Adam had to catch a plane to Philadelphia, and Lightning insisted we park the car and go into the terminal.

Several times in the waiting area, Adam and Lightning kissed. I walked over to read the flight schedule, appearing to be giving them space alone, but really because I was embarrassed. Finally everyone boarded. It was two minutes to departure. They embraced and kissed again. I continued to read the flight times but really remembering what I had written a week before in this chapter. I wrote "At an airport, a long hug and a light kiss can be appropriate." Now I was faced with that reality.

"Maybe if they just did a lighter kiss," I wondered.

"Hey, Roger, aren't you going to hug Adam goodbye?"

I clinched my teeth, tensed a bit, and walked over for a three-way embrace. Adam kissed Lightning one more time, then a light kiss for me. As Adam boarded, I looked around. No-one had paid any attention. No-one was offended. Only my own fear was the victim of their unabashed and open love.

On the way home I asked Lightning how he felt kissing in public. "It would be harder not to kiss a lover goodbye than to worry what others think," he answered. That was food for thought. I knew I had a lot to learn about *The Public Pat.*

## THE PUBLIC PAT
### Showing Comfortable Public Affection

*When you are with a friend or someone you love, give that person an unoffensive touch signifying your connection. The circumstances dictate the appropriateness. At an airport, a long hug and a light kiss might be right. At the Ritz, perhaps only a squeeze on the arm is comfortable. These are not just for public display, but primarily for us to show genuine thoughts of public love without fear, so they will bounce back to influence our lives.*

# CHAPTER FOURTEEN

# *Homosex*

Sex is undeniably a significant part of our lives. Sigmund Freud characterized its importance in everyday psychological feelings. Perhaps he overemphasized its role. Perhaps not. We at least know that the role of sex is profound.

Even our choice of friends has seemed to involve sexual orientation, or at least sexual tolerance. Our most intimate friends are usually also gay and lesbian. Our close non-gay friends are at the very least open-minded to accept us as we are.

We gay men and lesbians have a very close connection, and often the bonding between our two genders is solely because we are sexually different. That is enough to form our community. This is not to imply that sexual orientation is the only attraction between us. Nevertheless, we have all experienced a closeness with other people for no other apparent reason than they are all homosexuals.

We can not separate our spirituality from our sexuality. They don't compartmentalize. In a sense they are each part of the homogenized milk of our totality. We can neither take a pair of tweezers and separate the water from the solids in the milk, nor take sex out of our spirituality.

We all chose to be lesbian women, gay men, heterosexual, or bisexual, but much sooner than many think. Most of us know our sexual orientation from day one. For some people it may take half a lifetime to recognize it, but when it dawns, they know it was always there. If it was always there, then how could we choose to be homosexual or heterosexual?

We can not examine spirituality and sex without introducing the subject of reincarnation. I was in the closet on reincarnation much longer than I was in the closet sexually. When my music teacher introduced me to spiritual knowledge, including reincarnation, I immediately tried to share my new discoveries with my peers, only to be made fun of. I retried and retried, usually with the same put-down. Even in college as president of the Methodist Youth Fellowship, I tried to organize a special program on reincarnation. The reception was so cool I climbed into a closet corner and slammed the door. Not until I was thirty eight in Switzerland with a group learning to teach Transcendental Meditation did I crawl out and feel safe.

You should also understand that *life before birth* doesn't have to mean the life was on earth. There are an infinite number of other places to live. Some of them are where there is full Self-realization. Others, like the earth, have inhabitants that barely realize anything of their true nature. Since we're going through a major shift in awareness on earth now, this planet is almost over-loaded with souls that came for a rare chance of rapid enlightenment.

Because of this *phase-transition,* many of us came—not for our own enlightenment—but to help out. More on this in Chapter 17 where we discuss *Why Are We Here?*

The fears about sharing the concepts of reincarnation still linger. Perhaps I'm too sensitive to normal Christian attitudes. Nevertheless, the Truth of life after life after life is a cornerstone in metaphysics. That concept is also a cornerstone for understanding our sexual orientation.

Before we came into this life, each of us decided, with the loving guidance of wonderful Masters, what we each would emphasize. Some of us may have decided to come this time for our own growth, while others of us may have decided to serve. Then, like packing for any trip, we picked out which qualities and traits to bring. We are, after all, everything that is Mother/Father God, so we have an infinite variety to pick from. For some reason we lesbians, gay men, and even bisexuals chose to bring in a slight variation for our sexuality. Whatever the reason, we did it because it would fit us best for what we wanted to do. That sexual variation is not a shortcoming!! It results from our conscious decision for maximum results in our goals for this life.

Being a gay man, a lesbian, or a heterosexual is only for this lifetime, unless it is chosen again for another. We are totally sexual and totally asexual at the soul level—our Higher Self. At the soul level gay men, lesbians, and non-gays have all of the same qualities. For everyone, however, sexuality is expressed in particular ways in this lifetime for maximum good. Those are key words. *For everyone! For Maximum good!*

If we look closely at our own lives, we can see the role sex has played and is playing. Our choice of friends, our close relationships, our choice of careers, our choice of abodes, our choice of cities, our recreation, our spirituality— all these and more are a product of our sexuality. In every case, sex has compelled us into specific directions, and a specific life-style. It has all been for maximum good in the long haul. When that finally dawns, none of us could possibly want to be anyone else, or even to be ourselves with a different set of traits and qualities. We are perfectly equipped now for what we came to accomplish.

Total acceptance of our sexuality is a giant step in Self-acceptance. Accepting that we are a unique expression of God right now, yet at the same time that we are infinitely everything, is the grand realization. Everyone, whether gay or non-gay, is sexually unique, and that is the backdrop for Self-acceptance.

Sexuality and spirituality are meant to be married. To be spiritual is to be sexual. To be sexual is to be spiritual. To be spiritual and sexual is to be *spirexual*. I love that word. It says it all.

There are many, many ideas on sex, and it seems that many are denials of it. Even the practices linked to spiritual disciplines seem to inhibit full sexual expression. I've been admonished not to "waste my seed." I've been told by close friends that allowing sexual energies to be expressed robs my aura of light. One of those friends binds his penis at night in cheese cloth to inhibit an erection and wet dreams. I've been told I could have sex, but only without a climax. I actually tried that only to have to go to a doctor for a prostate problem. His remedy: an ejaculation three times a day for a week!!

I'm sure that all the various rules and practices do have their place for some people. They do not, however, have universal application. Instead we need a set of simple guidelines so that our spirituality and our sexuality do indeed marry and stay married.

Such guidelines would include non-judgment. We must be without judgment. We must accept everyone as unique and perfect, free to find and to express sex in any way he or she feels comfortable. We do this without thinking how strange, even in our private-most thoughts. If Mark feels he needs to bind his penis in cheese cloth, so be it. If Margaret is celibate, we accept that for her. If Monty uses tantra sex, we accept that for him. If George appears promiscuous, we don't judge. If Paul only has sex anonymously, we understand. If Beatrice and Emily celebrate fifty years of monogamy, we believe it. If mom and dad only use the missionary position, we don't snicker. Furthermore, we are without judgment about ourselves. We accept and love our sexual expressions, however, they come out, as long as they do not interfere with or do harm to others.

Guidelines would also include spirituality. We must bring spirituality into our unique sexual expressions. All the spirexual experiences we've learned can be applied in our sex lives.

In the sex act itself, always strive to feel *The Love Connection*. It may not always be there, but go into the act with that in mind. Whether a one night stand, a lover, or a spouse, let your awareness be with the feelings of love that can bubble up. Focus on them. They're your feelings, of course, but the sex act is the catalyst for them. Afterward, lie quietly together and let those feelings gel. Sex can truly be a love connection, but it will require your intention and focus.

During the sex act, let your thoughts be with those precious spirexual experiences *The Love Meltdown* and *Our Creator Connection*. By lying together in an embrace, you set up the perfect time to think, "I give you my love, I give you my heart, I receive your love, I receive your heart." Then wallow in the feelings of being unified together. Feel them well up, and well up they will.

While making love, think frequently of God's qualities for the two of you. "We are love, we are happiness, we are all-knowing intelligence." Use any qualities that come to you. These thoughts are your own, not to be shared, but your partner feels their effects. They are indeed felt.

Remember *The Beautiful Beatitude*. Let it become an integral part of sex. Whisper the beauty of your lover and your love-making experience.

Spiritual sex emphasizes the feelings of love, knowing that you're feeling what Einstein labeled the unified field, the most elementary energy in creation. We can make a conscious effort to cultivate those feelings of love with sex. At the same time we can use sex to unify with all of creation by recognizing our own and our partner's qualities. Even if we don't feel like thinking those qualities, we know them and feel them when we're having sex.

Guidance on what is your best sexual expression and even your best partners is always available. Develop the spirexual experience of *Channeling Your Higher Self.* This is your best ally in knowing everything you want and need to know about sex. After all, you can't read a book written by someone else on everything you need to know now about your sex life. No-one else can tell you what that is for you, but your Higher Self can. All the answers are within.

The hallmark of spiritual sex is that it is very simple, and we need not complicate it. These basic guidelines help to keep it simple, while emphasizing the love it is meant to bring into our lives.

However you choose to express sex, know it is your choice and not a mistake of nature. Know your sexual orientation is only for good. At the same time be without judgment about the many legitimate ways other people express sex. We are all unique expressions of the infinite, and how each of us expresses the infinite contributes to the beautiful collage of life: unity in diversity—diversity in unity.

# CHAPTER FIFTEEN

## *Manifesting Your True Desires*

In a sense we have been building up to this chapter. That is not to imply the previous experiences are only stepping stones. They are all complete and valuable in their own right. Neither does that imply this chapter is somehow the end product of all the knowledge. I mean only that the other spirexual experiences are now a foundation to manifest your true desires.

This chapter unfolds knowledge that is really the beginning. It is where we start from now on to bring about the world we truly want. Knowledge on how to manifest is our seed for happiness, prosperity, love, awareness, perfect health, a great job, homosexual respect—literally everything.

We are made in the image of our creator, God. He/She is truly our Mother/Father. All we are, and all that is, is a creation of God. God is undeniably a creator, and being made in that image, we are also creators.

God's creation began with His/Her thought—a clear vision of what was to be created. That thought stirred the unified field—the infinite, that unmanifest sea of sleeping energy, love—to materialize in the variety of shapes and personalities of the universe. It all began with His/Her thought.

Being made in God's image, we create in the same way. We think, and we stir those infinite energies of the unified field. In that way, we draw to us whatever we think. Nature assumes that what we think is what we want. Nature's energies are without judgment. They don't double check what we say or think. We are free to ask for whatever we want to experience, and what we ask for we get.

Therefore, if you don't like your life, it is because you are not stating what you truly desire. Somehow there is a lack of communication.

We do not need to learn how to manifest. We have that down pat. We just think. It's that simple, and we already know how to think.

Sometimes we're thinking on automatic, so we don't even hear our thoughts. That's the subconscious, and it's extremely valuable. It is given to us so we can automatically program our mind to ask for those things we always want. That way we won't be overburdened by constantly thinking about what to manifest. We want instead to use our time to enjoy life.

That automatic program is our responsibility. Neither God, nor our mothers, nor our lovers, nor our third grade teachers, nor TV actors, nor anyone else put that programming there. We did, perhaps at their suggestion. Nevertheless, we put it there, and we can change it.

The experience for creating our true desires is not a way to mechanically reach into the ethers to pull out an orange, or whatever. *The Creating Formula* is a way to think. If we think correctly, we can create and experience anything.

*The Creating Formula* is a simple seven-part sentence: *GOD AND I CLAIM AND ACCEPT*

*THOUGHTS WITH FORGIVENESS AND THANKS,
AMEN.*

The sentence has no cosmic meaning, but each word represents one of the seven steps:

1. GOD
2. I
3. CLAIM AND ACCEPT
4. THOUGHTS
5. FORGIVENESS
6. THANKS
7. AMEN

Each word is an important part of the formula, and all parts together give us a foolproof vehicle to experience whatever we desire. A common desire many of us seem to have is to have a lover—to share the love experience with another person. Let's use that desire and go through each of the seven steps to illustrate *The Creating Formula.*

### *1. GOD*

Start the formula with *The Creator Connection.* That is, begin by thinking Mother/Father God's qualities. That elevates your thinking to that level. Feel that process and continue thinking some of God's qualities until you clearly feel the love of God. There are no particular words here to memorize. However, by way of example, you might think:

*"God is love. God is light, Truth. God is happiness, joy, and bliss. God is all-knowing intelligence. God is everywhere present. God is perfection. God is peace and gentleness. God is infinite energy. God is abundance. God is without judgment."*

### *2. I*

After you feel the love of God, recognize that you are made in the image of God, that you are one with God, and that God's qualities are yours. Continue to repeat these qualities until you think of them as your own. That is the feeling of being unified. An example of this section is:

*"I am made in the image of God. I am made with those same qualities that God has. I am one with God. Therefore, I am love. I am light, Truth. I am happiness, joy, and bliss. I am all-knowing intelligence. I am also everywhere present. I am perfection. I am peace and gentleness. I am infinite energy. I am abundance. I am without judgment."*

### 3. CLAIM AND ACCEPT

This section is what you desire. It is always in the present tense. It is always as specific as possible, and always what you presently believe you can achieve, because you must believe to create. If you doubt, that simply means there is another thought more powerful that is still doing the creating. For instance, if you claim to earn a million dollars next year, you would probably doubt it. Such a powerful doubt would thwart your getting the money. You need to begin with the believable. Slowly, what you believe expands. Then one day you realize that you have no doubts, and literally anything you claim becomes yours.

You only want to claim your true desires, and there is only one foolproof way to find out what they are. Ask. Your Higher Self knows your true desires. Remember, you came into this life for a particular purpose. You came with all the tools, talents, and equipment to succeed. It would be a waste of time striving for success in a Stuffed Potato restaurant if you came to be a teacher. Likewise, you may be better able to accomplish your goals by living alone at this time, even though you dream of having a lover. If you were to start the restaurant (as I once did), or take on a lover when it is not in your highest interest, you would quickly feel frustrated. Underneath everything, you are most determined to succeed at your highest goals, even if that means knocking down roadblocks you put up. Therefore, always channel your Higher Self to learn your true desires before making a claim.

If your Higher Self verifies it is your true desire to have a lover, your claim might be:

*"I claim that I am a lover to the perfect man/woman to experience love together."*

You must also accept what you've claimed. Many of our thoughts leave this out. If you don't accept, you'll never get. It's that simple. You can wish for lovers "from now 'til kingdom come," but if you refuse to accept them, they can't manifest. The UPS is willing to deliver. Will you accept the package? To accept, say:

*"I accept that I am a lover to the perfect man/woman to experience love together."*

You can be abundant in your claims, so whenever possible, add the words "or better" in any Claim and Acceptance. The desire can be fulfilled in an entirely different way from what you expect, and you have to be open to that. When you say "or better" or the equivalent, you allow yourself that possibility.

## 4. THOUGHTS

This is the section to deal with your thoughts that hinder your claim. It won't do any good to claim and accept a lover if you have powerful overriding thoughts that say, "I don't deserve a lover," or "I'm afraid of intimacy," or "No-one could ever want me to love." There are countless such error beliefs that need to be erased. Some are conscious. Most are subconscious. Who knows, or even cares, why you put such false notions in your program. You need to discover them and then to change them.

Again, channel your Higher Self. This is your access to the vast subconscious. Ask what error beliefs are inhibiting your experience of a specific true desire. Using *Yes* and *No* signals as an aid, channel what the error beliefs are for each stated desire. The thoughts that inhibit your experience of the true desire could be fears, or doubts, or anger, or mistaken beliefs. They could be almost anything.

Once you recognize the error beliefs that hinder your claim, heal the thoughts and replace them with the correct thoughts. Heal by simply stating that you heal and release the erroneous thought about such and such. The error belief is then replaced with the correct Truth. In the lover example, this section could be like this:

*"I heal and release the erroneous thought that no-one would ever want me for a lover. In Truth I am a perfect, beautiful, and loving person that many people find attractive and would want for a lover. I also heal and release the erroneous thought that I am afraid of intimacy. In Truth I am a loving person created in God's image along with everyone else. It is safe and natural for me to be physically and emotionally near other people, and I can not be harmed in any way by intimacy with others."*

When all the error beliefs you know about are healed, released, and replaced, end this section with:

*"I heal and release all thoughts I may have that interfere with this claim, known or unknown, conscious or subconscious. My thoughts are now one with, the same as, and in tune with, God's thought."*

### 5. FORGIVENESS

Often grudges you hold keep your true desires from coming about. This is really another aspect of error beliefs that needs healing, but grudges are so common that a separate section is warranted. No-one can hurt you because you are made perfect and always will be perfect. If you think someone has hurt you, or taken something from you, or infringed upon you in any way, it is because that is what you, as creator, invited. Often the people you continue to hold grudges against are forgotten, at least on the surface. In the subconscious you continue to hold the festering, the hurt, the disgust, the fear, or the anger toward people. These thoughts are devastating because they really are a denial of all that you are. How can you manifest as a perfect creator when you think someone can easily crack your shell of perfection?

Again, you must ask your Higher Self what people to forgive to clear the way for creating your true desire. You need not relive or reexamine each torrid incident. No, no, no!! That might just reinfect your mind. You just need to identify the people by name or picture. Then forgive in the way you learned with *The Forgiveness Formula*.

An example of forgiveness for the lover illustration might be:

*"Michael, my dear lover of years ago, I made a mistake in my thinking to allow you to seemingly hurt me. I recognize that you were*

*merely doing what I invited, and that in reality neither you nor anyone else can hurt me. I am perfect now, always have been, and always will be. You can't change that, and never did. I now recognize that life is for giving love to you and everyone. I give you my love."*

### 6. THANKS

In this section put your heart into a sea of gratitude. That emotion of thanks finishes the healing process. It opens your channels to allow nature to pour the experiences of your true desires to you. All this comes with a simple thanks. In our example, it could be:

*"I thank God that I am a lover to the perfect man/woman and that we experience love together.*

### 7. AMEN

This is *the end.* Let go of your claim. If you hold on, it's because you doubt the formula works. Don't desperately cling to the idea, looking for some sign this formula is working. That clinging is really a form of fear. Thus, in this section, just let go. An example is:

*"I release this claim to God and to natural laws of creation. My claim is now created. That is the nature of natural law. Amen."*

That's it. You can now create what you have channeled from your Higher Self to be your true desires. Life is not meant to be a struggle. If it is, you can easily create the simple, safe, loving life of your true desires.

## THE CREATING FORMULA
### Manifesting Your True Desires
### With Your Thoughts

*The purpose of the formula is to correct your thinking and create your true desires. The following sentence clues you for the seven parts of the formula: GOD AND I CLAIM AND ACCEPT THOUGHTS WITH FORGIVENESS AND THANKS, AMEN.*

### 1. GOD
*Unify with God by reciting His/Her qualities.*
### 2. I
*Raise your awareness to your Higher Self by reciting your God qualities.*
### 3. CLAIM AND ACCEPT
*Claim a true desire (or better) as verified by channeling your Higher Self. Then, accept the creation of that true desire.*
### 4. THOUGHTS
*Correct any erroneous beliefs, fears, doubts, or anger that your Higher Self tells you stands in the way of experiencing your true desire.*
### 5. FORGIVENESS
*Heal any grudges you hold against people your Higher Self tells you stands in the way of experiencing your true desire. Use The Forgiveness Formula.*
### 6. THANKS
*Feel gratitude to God and nature for bringing you the experience of your true desire.*
### 7. AMEN
*Release and let go.*

117

## *Channeling Our Masters*

We no longer ever need to doubt that each of us is significant, regardless of sexual orientation. We no longer need to doubt that being gay or lesbian or heterosexual fits perfectly into our life goals. If doubt still lingers, we now have accumulated enough knowledge and experiences to channel our Masters on these and every other subject.

Wherever we are, we are surrounded by our Masters. Our homes, the countryside, downtown, and our workshops are teaming with Masters. It is literally impossible to be without them.

It would easier to remove all oxygen from the universe than to remove the Masters from every nook and cranny. They are omnipresent. The universe is their body. They are with us and at the same time with everyone else. Just because a Master is gently guiding one of us does not preclude him or her from guiding someone else at the same time. Time and space do not exist as we know them in the Master's abode. The Masters are not bound by the here and the now. They are limitless.

Of course, these are our own qualities in Truth as well. We have chosen this trip to earth in the twentieth century, and that is our focus. Beyond that focus we are also omnipresent, and the universe is also our body.

When a diver looks into the clear ocean from a ship before diving to a treasure below, his mission is clear. He can see the treasure clearly, and he knows exactly what to do. After diving the water gets cloudy, and he gets disoriented, and he forgets some of his plans. The life chord to the ship on the surface links him to the overall mission. His fellow workmen are there to guide him. "More to the left," "There's a shark in the area, prepare to surface," or "Just take inventory on this dive."

Of course, the diver can ignore the advice from the ship, and he can even disconnect his link. Then he is left alone to figure out what he's doing there and how to do it all by himself. That does not change reality. The ship and his fellow crew members are still there and still trying to help. When he resurfaces, everything becomes clear again.

On our dive into this thick atmosphere, we have lost some memory of who we are and why we came. Like the diver, we also have a link to reality and to our friends who see clearly all about creation.

Our friends are the enlightened Masters. They have full awareness. They see and speak only Truth. Many of them never left that awareness once they were created. Others lost the light and pulled themselves back by learning and experiencing, much like most people on earth are now doing. How a Master became a Master is not important. We are only concerned that the Master is indeed enlightened—that he or she perceives the whole picture and can give us Truth.

Some Masters are on earth now in a physical body, and some are only in the spiritual realm. Those with us in the physical are often the most unsuspecting. With a very special mission, they may have chosen to leave behind some memory of who they are and where they came from. This is necessary so they will fit into society easily and not be separate. I have no doubt that many of you are Masters, even though you may not give yourself that label.

The Masters we wish to contact are the ones who are totally aware of their Master status and role. Whether or not they presently also have a physical body is immaterial. They are the Masters that are with us at all times, like the crew on the ship. They are constantly whispering guidance, encouragement, and love. We do hear them.

*Channeling Our Masters* is nothing new. We've done it from birth without realizing it. Now we can channel the Masters with clarity, certainty, confidence, and full awareness. Knowing the source, we can rely and act on the guidance.

Which of the Masters do you want to hear? Jesus? Buddha? Saint Francis? Mary? Babaji? Yogananda? Krishna? You can name any you want. And it's likely you'll also hear from some you don't recognize yet.

*Channeling Our Masters* is like *Channeling Your Higher Self*. Get into a meditative state, then ask for a Master to give you his or her signal. You can specify a Master, or ask for the most appropriate one. You can also contact several, getting a different signal for each.

These signals are similar to those for your Higher Self, so expect any movement, sensation, feelings, visions, or anything else you'd notice that is pleasant. When you clearly have the signal and feel comfortable with it, speak out the thoughts given to you by the Master, verifying periodically with your *Yes* and *No* signals. You can also use your *Yes* and *No* signals to ask questions. All the rules and procedures you've used in *Channeling Your Higher Self* are applicable. After all, we are also Masters at the level of our Higher Selves.

*Channeling Our Masters* can be your tool to receive any knowledge you desire that is your highest and wisest interest to know. This is not to imply that we don't have the same Truth available with our Higher Selves. We certainly do. *Channeling Our Masters* is simply another variation, with the side benefit of being able to experience specific flavors of the love energy each of the Masters radiates.

Perhaps when more and more of us develop these experiences, we can freely exchange the lessons and knowledge we've received from Buddha, Jesus, Babaji, or Mary without batting an eye. It certainly would be easy—and fun!

Here's another suggestion. Ask the Master to give you a hug. You will definitely feel something. Loneliness and even depression are overshadowed by the feeling of being loved. Just ask for a hug.

Some of the most delightful evenings I've had with gay friends were spent *Channeling Our Masters* together. We used a guided group meditation which incorporates and teaches many of the tools you now find is second nature. The procedure for this group experience is exact and was channeled to me by the Master Babaji.

One person in the group acts as a moderator and stays alert to read the instructions, keep track of time, and to observe that everything is going smoothly. For fifteen people, allow about two hours for this channeling so you have time to share experiences afterward. Don't try to have a larger group than fifteen, but of course any number less would be fine.

The words are to be exactly spoken as given, and the time periods between instructions are not arbitrary. I know this precise format does give the desired results, so do not deviate or improvise.

After arranging the group into a circle, the leader begins to read the instructions:

"I'm your guide for your conscious contact with the teaching Masters. As you know, we are going to channel from some of the great Masters knowledge they think is in our highest interest to receive. The first thing each of you needs to do is to think of some Master you know about that you would enjoy communicating with. It can be any you want to hear from: Jesus, Buddha, Krishna, Mary, St. Francis, Babaji, Yogananda, or any others you have in mind. You can also just open yourself up to allow the perfect Master for you to appear. This is going to be a meditation type of experience, so let's begin by closing the eyes. In your own way, get centered and relaxed."

*(one minute)*

"We close our auras to all except the vibration of our Higher Selves. We surround ourselves with white light, and we receive Truth only through that light. Let's remember we are made in the image of our creator. That means we have the same qualities as our creator. I'm going to express a few of those qualities. After each one, repeat silently the quality as your own. Love.

*(Pause after each quality.)* Light. Happiness, joy, and bliss. All knowing intelligence. Present everywhere for all time. Perfection. Peace and gentleness. Infinite energy. Abundance. Without judgment. Timeless.

"Now breath normally, but connect your breath. That is, there is no space between the inhale and the exhale. The breath is like a round wheel. Just without effort let this connected breathing carry itself. Keep your attention on your breathing."

*(one minute)*

"Easy, effortless breathing. It is okay to have thoughts along with the awareness of the breath. Just slightly favor the awareness of the breath."

*(two minutes)*

"Easy, effortless breathing. If your mind is off on a thought, gently come back to the awareness of the breath."

*(one minute)*

"Easy, effortless breathing." *(repeat every minute)*

*(seven minutes)*

"Now breath normally without trying to connect your breath. Allow your attention to be with your heart. Just feel your heart and notice the feelings in that region."

*(two minutes)*

"Do you notice a pulsation in the heart region that is not from the heart beat?"

*(three minutes)*

"Raise your finger if you notice a pulsation in that heart region that is not from the heart beat? *(pause)* Very good. Continue to notice that pulsation in the heart region."

*(five minutes)*

"Now raise your finger if you notice a pulsation in the heart region that is not from the heart beat."

*(short pause)*

"Very good. That is the signal from the Master. If you don't feel it yet, don't be concerned. Now we are going to ask for a more physical signal. Sit comfortably, so that your arms, fingers, legs are free to move. Your head should be able to pivot, like the little doggie in the car window. Don't touch the back of the chair, so your back can move. Now silently ask the Master to give you some physical signal of his or her presence."

*(short pause)*

"The signal can be anything you can notice. It can be a movement, or some sensation, or some vision. Anything you can notice. When you receive the signal, share it with the rest of us, along with the name of the Master. If your heart pulsation that isn't the heart beat remains prominent, you may wish that to be your only signal."

*(ten minutes)*

"Now you are going to channel out loud your Master. Be open and receptive to your Master and feel his or her love in your heart. We close our auras to all except our Christ vibrations. We receive knowledge now only through The Light. Hold with you at all times during your channeling the signal from your Master.

"When someone else is channeling out loud, you may find that you have another distinct signal for the Master being channeled. You may also feel a distinct flavor of love from each of the Masters we hear from.

"Channeling your Master is neither flashy nor out of the ordinary. In your thoughts your

Master places seed ideas. You speak out these ideas in your own words. For now, you can most easily recognize the seed ideas because they will be general statements of Truth. It may even appear to you that you are making up what you want to say. That's why you keep the Master's signal with you at all times you're speaking out.

"When you begin, state your name, the name of the Master, and what your signal is. Then simply speak out whatever the seed thoughts are. When you are finished, tap the person to your right, and that person continues. The person on my right will now begin."

*(complete the circle once)*

"Let's take at least two minutes now to gradually open our eyes. Stretch, massage, or whatever is natural for you. Do this slowly. If you hurry, you might feel some irritability for a short time."

*(at least two minutes)*

"Would anyone like to share his or her experience?"

### CHANNELING OUR MASTERS
*Receiving Truth And Guidance*
*From Our Masters*

*Use the same procedures and guidelines as in Channeling Your Higher Self. Ask for and get a signal for each Master you wish to channel. Then channel or ask questions in precisely the same way you do for your Higher Self.*

# CHAPTER SEVENTEEN

## Why Are We Here?

When I was preparing for a workshop of gay men, I was thunderstruck with a strong message that kept surfacing in my channeling with one of our Masters. Although it made sense to me, I felt strange in sharing it because it is very different from anything I had heard. Nevertheless, I did share it with the men, and to my surprise, they too felt comfortable. You've read this far, so these pages might have special significance for you also.

This message is for a certain group of gay men, lesbians, and enlightened heterosexuals. Our number is very large and scattered all over the earth. Although there are more non-gays in sheer numbers, a larger percentage of the homosexual population is in this group. Our priorities and life style are such that we can more easily do our work as gay men and lesbians. That's one reason we chose our sexuality, and it is an important ingredient.

We really are an incredible group of men and women. We have lived on earth many times. We love it here. Earth is a gorgeous being, and we know her intimately. At some point a shadow of ignorance fell upon mankind here. For many of us, that was in the latter days of Atlantis. We saw greed and misuse of power destroy our civilization. To escape the inevitable destruction

126

and to preserve the sacred knowledge, we migrated to Egypt and Mexico where we took our technology, the crystal power, and Truth about our Selves.

Eventually, even these outposts fell victim to the darkness, which has lasted to this time. In biblical terms, this was the original sin. It's actually the only sin, if we can label anything sin. Humankind had forgotten the Self.

Because we had heightened awareness, and because the people on earth had fallen into ignorance, we moved to another star system. Moving was as simple as focusing on your finger, then the toe. After all, the whole universe is our body, and we can enjoy any aspect or part we want to focus on.

Now there is a chance to awaken humanity on this planet. A window in time has opened, and the possibility for a new dawning is here. Because of this rare chance, billions of souls from other unenlightened planets and star systems have converged here. Their own Higher Selves knew of the possiblity to discard forever the chains of ignorance about the Self.

However, the opportunity to awaken is just a possibility. Much work needs to be done, and that's why we volunteered to come back. Without extensive help, it would be nearly impossible for these souls to become enlightened. There are just too many errors in mass-consciousness to be corrected. Much negativism needs to be neutralized. Vibrations need to be raised several octaves. There is really only one effective way all this could be accomplished quickly with certainty. The window of time doesn't last forever. Large numbers of enlightened people had to come to the earth to work.

That's why we're here. We knew we would loose memory of who we are and where we came from so we could easily melt right into society. Earth is a dear place to us, and we've wanted since leaving to awaken humankind here to the reality of the Self. Our work is such that we couldn't know our origin and do the work effectively. Hopefully, though, this little bit of insight will give us the courage and energy to continue with diligence.

We also knew our work wouldn't be easy. No-one has thrust this experience upon us. We knew clearly at one point exactly what we were getting into. With full informed consent we volunteered.

There are three roles we each have, and we all seem to be carrying these out to some degree. The first role is to unify often in any way we feel comfortable at least once each day. To unify is simply to bring our awareness to our Self. That connects us to God, to creation, to Truth, and to everyone else on earth. Where we came from, being unified is a continuous state of mind. In this thick earth atmosphere we fall under the influence of life on earth. Being unified is not a continuous reality here at this time. We must be constantly reminded until being unified is a natural state for everyone. Every time we unify, we pull all people here up a notch closer to full Self-realization because *we are all one.*

There are many ways to unify. I'm sure every person reading this has a favorite technique. Let's neither be judgmental about someone else's technique, nor think ours is the only one or the best, any more than we think our own sexual expression is best. Each is guided to the most natural for him or her. We have to crack this nut by hitting it on all sides; that's why we see so many different ways in which people unify.

Some people unify with deep meditation. Others insist their meditation is swimming laps or running. A long walk is my father's meditation. A whole host of physical and mental exercises all have as a goal the awareness of the Self. Pick your favorites. You'll be drawn to them. Then be generous in allotting time for being unified. It's one of our supreme roles.

The spirexual experiences are also to unify. *The Conscious Connection, Channeling Your Higher Self,* and *Channeling Our Masters* are grand meditations that unify and tickle the earth and everyone here with Truth. *The Love Meltdown* unifies our heart, as does *The Love Connection* and *Our Creator Connection.* Feeling *The Soul Site* zeroes our awareness to our core and unifies.

The group experiences of *Channeling Our Masters* and *The Mass-Consciousness Correction* also unify. Surface experiences of *The Beautiful Beatitude* and *The Public Pat* also have their unifying effect. Every time we use any of these spirexual experiences, we are forever changing humankind. Use them frequently, and incorporate any others you run into that seem appropriate and comfortable.

The second role we all have is to just be. We are all antennas for very powerful cosmic energies. They are being transmitted to the earth now by our dear enlightened friends on the other side. These cosmic energies carry knowledge of the infinite that is coded and complete. Humankind has always had these energies around, but they have been refused.

When a television set is turned on, it receives the incoming signal and a dark tube lights up for all to see what the signal carries. By the same token, our physical nervous systems are receivers for cosmic energy. We turn on, so to speak, and the signals are received. Then we splash all over the planet without effort what the cosmic energy brings. No-one can escape its influence. People are being deluged with love, and "ah-ha" experiences, and with healing rays.

Being this antenna is our easiest job. There's nothing to do or think. Just be. Of course, the voltage can be quite strong at times. Have you noticed? Just remember, we volunteered, knowing it wouldn't be easy.

The third role we all have is to dissipate negativism that is in the earth atmosphere from eons of strife here or that was brought by billions of souls from another place. This is the one role that is definitely not comfortable, but someone has to do it. We all have many different ways to do this, as any cursory glance reveals. There are, however, three basic categories for dissipating negativism. Over the course of a lifetime, we each participate in all three categories, some more than others.

One way to dissipate negativism is to take on false beliefs and then come to grips with them. How often we've all heard, "I no sooner work through one layer than another appears. Will they never stop?"

We've all assumed we were working on our own stuff. Well, surprise! It seems like our own stuff, but it's really part of the scum in this barrel that needs to be cleaned out. When we take on a false belief and work through it in our own lives, we forever change mass-consciousness to some degree. It accomplishes this due to our interconnectedness.

There are thousands of false beliefs, and we're all nibbling away at several each. The issue of *poverty consciousness* is classic. Few seem to escape this one because so many of humankind's values are rooted in it. When we remember we are abundance by nature and that all creative energy flows through us at our command, the false belief crumbles.

*Being loved* is another big issue. Somehow humankind got the idea it is a struggle to be loved. Doubts about deserving love crept in. Loneliness was born. Well, loneliness is an illusion, so many of us have taken on the love issue. When we tackle it, we help dissipate the negativism associated with lack of love.

You could probably write an entire book on your stuff. You know what it is. Even if you think it truly is your stuff, it doesn't matter. By coming to grips with it, you forever alter mass-consciousness. Be grateful, therefore, for this opportunity to make a meaningful mark with your life.

A second way we dissipate negativism is to allow it to come to us, then neutralize it with love. That's what I experienced on Cape Cod with the gay-bashing insults. When someone screams at you, silently send them *The Love Meltdown:* "I give you my love, I give you my heart, I receive your love, I receive your heart." Then remove yourself without getting involved.

Whenever we experience verbal negativism come to us, what is being said is not what is being meant. Remember that. It will be a lot easier to stay detached and not get sucked in. If someone screams he hates you, be well assured the words are meaningless. All you can know is that person is experiencing turmoil and discomfort. This can be dispelled to a great extent by *The Love Meltdown*. It always has an effect. Always. So impulse it, and then leave the region fast. We don't deserve to be deluged with nastiness.

For awhile we can all expect to get our share of negativism. Neutralizing it is one of our major roles, it seems, and we can now quickly do just that. Just keep in mind the divine purpose of what you're doing, and it'll be easier.

The last category for dissipating negativism is the most difficult to talk about There are none of us not involved in some way. In this role, we use our bodies as sponges. We let our bodies absorb negativism, even to the point of serious illness. AIDS is one such illness, but by no means the only one. It is like cleaning up chicken litter, using our bodies as wipers. We wouldn't have agreed to this if it weren't absolutely necessary. We did so because there is a huge pile of the "litter" and the method is quite efficient.

The negativism still around the earth is overwhelming. There are deadly wars. We're still contaminating the air. We're still destroying the ozone layers. We're still poisoning our water. We're still generating tons of deadly nuclear waste. We're still cutting down the rain forests. We're still hating in the name of God and religion. And so it goes.

It is also clear that tremendous changes are taking place. We indeed are clearing out the negativism. International cooperation is improving beyond our wildest hopes. Whole societies are reclaiming their power and cultural identity. People are demanding respect for the environment and natural systems. There is growing awareness of individual rights and human dignity—the first step in recognizing the oneness of the Self.

The task ahead is still enormous, so we're pulling out all stops. As long as there is a minuscule of a chance for our fellow humans to be enlightened, we will do everything we can as individuals and as a group.

When our bodies absorb the negativism, we do, of course, get sick. Sometimes we can flush it out, like ringing out a cleaning cloth. If we keep absorbing negativism into our bodies, as some of us have agreed to do, we'll reach the saturation point and drop the body. We see this happening all around us, and to say it isn't easy is the understatement of the millennium.

In addition to our general roles of unifying, of receiving cosmic energies, and of dissipating negativism, each of us also has our own particular work to do. Some of us are introducing whole new legal concepts. Others are organizing environmental groups to save the animals, the atmosphere, the forests, and our waters. Many are working from within business to correct "polluting mentality" and to change ethics. Civil rights causes need their leaders and workers. Holistic health care is gaining ground, as is our concern about what we eat. These need exponents. Every place we turn we see inroads into that stale mass-consciousness, and many of the inroads have been made by our group. As we change thinking, others pick up and run with the new concepts.

Some of the specific work we do is far reaching in its influence. More than likely, however, it is quite ordinary and unnoticed. It doesn't matter.

We don't need to fret over what is best to do; we simply need to do for the moment whatever seems natural. Then we will be fulfilling our divine mission as lesbians, gay men, and enlightened heterosexuals.

Yes, we are an incredible group of men and women. We have come as the road crew to pave the way for an enlightened age. We can't imagine now the tremendous significance of our lives, but we will. Then we can only be proud we came.

CHAPTER EIGHTEEN

## *AIDS*

I won a drawing at the YMCA for two airline tickets to Hawaii. "I hope you have someone special to take," the membership director said, half inquiring. Indeed I did. Considering Drew's class schedule and the dates that were blocked out by the airline, we found only one window when we could go—the last two weeks in August.

I got every travel brochure, book, and map I could find. I read, pondered, and talked Hawaii, until finally Drew made me promise not to mention it until two weeks before departure. It was hard, but I managed to be quiet, while continuing my own excursion into the fantasy.

Finally we could talk about it, and I brought out the maps, pictures, suggested itinerary, car options, camping spots, luaus, gay bars, nude beaches—you name it, I had it. The excitement started to boil over. The next morning, Drew woke up with a 103 fever, cold sweats, aches, diarrhea, and no appetite.

"Thank God he has the flu before our trip," we thought. "Better now than in Lahaina."

Doug called and confirmed our diagnosis as flu. He'd just spent four days as sick as he'd ever been. Another friend also had the same symptoms. We counted the days, but on the fifth he was still sick, loosing weight, and exhausted. Suspecting Rocky Mountain Spotted Fever, his doctor gave him antibiotics, but after two days the symptoms remained.

I will never forget the sinking feeling I got late on the seventh night when his doctor called. I listened on the extension as he said, "Drew, I strongly suspect you have AIDS. I want you to check into the student infirmary tonight so we can start some tests in the morning."

Drew hung up. We starred at each other. Tears welled up for both of us. "I think he's right," Drew whispered. I put my arms around him, and we both broke down.

I think I have an extraordinary view of birth, life, and death. I often appear very strong in crises, and I have been the Rock of Gibraltar for many people. But this? I wasn't prepared. There is no way to describe my sadness and my helplessness.

In spite of a negative HIV test several months earlier, the next three days seemed to bear out the doctor's suspicions. While driving or standing in line at the supermarket I found myself spontaneously crying. There is nothing anyone could say to me. It was a living nightmare. I was so overcome I almost forgot to cancel the Hawaii trip. All those plans seemed so trivial now.

Drew's story ended differently than many. Quit suddenly the fever broke, and his strength and appetite returned. His HIV test came back negative again and Drew came home. However, I shall always know the feelings of my dear brothers and sisters who have a loved-one with AIDS. I realize nothing can be said to ease the anguish, because what I have to say I already knew. The knowledge in this chapter didn't make it easier for me, even though I was dealing only with a possibility my lover had AIDS. Nevertheless, I am compelled to share it with you now.

Last year in Santa Fe, New Mexico, I volunteered to give the hands on healing treatments called Reiki to several AIDS patients. They were trying alternative remedies. I was struck by the beauty of the men. In their darkest moments, each seemed to exude light. They joked and kept a cheerful outlook. I don't mean they weren't often frightened, sad, or perplexed. They were. Yet, they had an underlying calmness.

I remember thinking more than once that I was in the midst of saints. Little did I realize how true that was until near the end of my volunteering. I was giving a treatment to Mark, a stunningly handsome man. We had a special connection, and we both admitted sexual attraction. I can remember the swirl of energy I'd feel when I augmented the Reiki with *The Love Meltdown.*

At one of those quiet special moments, I got my signal for one of the Masters. The message was clear. I heard it over and over and checked it with my *Yes* and *No* signals. I was indeed receiving a personal, yet universal, message for him.

"Mark," I said, "you are to know you are on a very significant and divine mission right now. It won't be easy, and you knew when you volunteered it wouldn't be easy. And you won't know or understand much while you're in the physical. Just know that everything is perfect and that you are right on course, doing a profound thing for the earth."

I paused, and I could see he was deep in thought. I asked, "Does that make sense to you?"

"Yes, it does," he whispered. Tears rolled down his cheeks. "Yes, it does. It all makes perfect sense now."

A few months later I was at a Sunday afternoon garden party. Terry showed a group of us around his spectacular grounds. As the group moved on, I noticed a young man staying behind on a bench. I walked up and introduced myself. He's John, a professional dancer, age 25, and originally from New York City. We were discussing his love for the garden when suddenly he looked into my eyes and quietly said, "I don't want to die."

Caught off guard, I awkwardly put my arms around him. There was nothing to say. I knew what he meant. Then, just like in Santa Fe, I received my signal from a Master with the strong impulse to share the same message with him that I received for Mark.

"John, we have come here for a special mission. Earth is not really our home now, but it used to be. There is so much ignorance and negative energy here, and one of our jobs is to help neutralize it. We do that in many ways, and some of us are allowing our bodies to absorb it. Then, when we have a full load, we drop the body. It's a really profound thing we're doing, and you're on the front line. It won't be easy, of course. But it is necessary, and it is profound."

"But my career was just getting started when I first came down with pneumonia," he said. "I don't want to die."

"Death and birth are synonyms," I answered. "When you were born, you gave up life somewhere else. When you give up this life, you'll start another back home where we came from. Birth and death are the same—it is just a matter of your vantage point whether you're dying or being born."

We walked quietly back to the house, arm in arm, for dinner. Later John took me aside and said, "You know, I think what you said is true. All this finally makes sense."

I would like to think this realization makes the disease easier. It doesn't seem to, although we do gain a certain perspective. Nothing about AIDS is easy.

Even the HIV test is difficult to take. Drew was determined to be tested when we lived in Santa Fe. I was just as adamant not to. I had long since lost count of my dear friends who had died, many of whom were my sex partners. I assumed I was a carrier of the virus so Drew and I would only have "safe sex." Drew felt intuitively we were not positive and wanted to know. He simply announced one day that he was getting tested with or without me.

I gave in, but the three week period for the results was agony. I kept reflecting on how Michael fell apart when he learned he was positive. Could I cope with a positive result? I honestly didn't know. With all of my metaphysical training and these wonderful spirexual experiences down pat, I still didn't know how I would react. After all, we are human. We have the full range of human emotion, and we need not try to kid ourselves. I'm sure a positive result would prey on my mind just like it does everyone else.

Both of our tests came back negative, but the fears haven't gone away. When Drew was suspected of having AIDS, I once again had to be tested. It was just as difficult.

Yes, this disease is life's most difficult time for many of us. Neutralizing negativism is not for sissies. We're shoveling away all the crap that's been building up for eons. It must go, or humankind will end up destroying the planet and God knows what else along with it.

Not everyone with AIDS is someone who came here specifically for that purpose. Those who did come for that purpose have nervous systems capable of neutralizing far more negativism, however. Yet everyone with the disease is helping to cleanse the atmosphere.

This is not meant to imply that neutralizing negativism is the only cosmic purpose for AIDS. It isn't. I have been with people who have had immense personal growth during the illness.

My friend John from the garden party went back to New York City during a remission. He healed a major rift with his parents. In the process he opened his heart and allowed them in. I know people who have spent a lifetime without releasing parental resentments, but he did it in one visit. He later returned to live with them.

Alex spent time letting go of illusions. His expensive car and fancy home were put into perspective. Jealousies over his lover withered away. Even a career that was his life blood didn't matter.

In Marty I saw a spiritual awakening. He was always too busy for concepts like God. Suddenly, almost overnight, he started talking about divine plans, about life after death, and about a "higher power," as he called it.

Warren was always head strong, aggressive, and determined. In his final weeks I saw a softening. He seemed to accept the inevitable, instead of being determined to change the impossible. He even joked about fate and expressed gratitude for whatever time could give him.

When I finally took my trip to Hawaii, I added an extra week to spend with my long time buddy George on The Big Island. He had just moved there to be with his closest friends after his first round in the hospital with AIDS. When I made arrangements, George was feeling great and full of life. I knew we'd have a wonderful time together.

I was totally unprepared for the dear friend I found. Thin, feverish, and weak, he had strength for only an hour visit. Before the week was over he was in the hospital. In spite of his condition, I am still awed by the insights he shared.

"This is a great period of tremendous growth," George told me. "Something I read said that health is really the balance between the head and the heart. When we have that then we just let the body do what it must do."

These men with AIDS experienced personal growth that might have taken lifetimes of ordinary living. The opportunity was there, and they used it.

Furthermore, let's not forget we also clean up mass-consciousness when we clean up our own error-filled thinking. Each of these men changed to some degree what everyone on earth thinks. Such a privilege it is for someone to help usher in the enlightened age!

To have this understanding about AIDS is not to suggest for a moment we give up on the disease. No. This is only to give us perspective. The pain isn't made less, only more tolerable. Those people with AIDS need to use every medical and metaphysical treatment available to prolong life and to be comfortable. This is part of the process. When enough global cleansing has taken place, a treatment will surface.

In anticipation of that time it is necessary that we as a group—indeed all of humanity—commit money and resources to wipe out AIDS. A time will quickly come when its specific purpose will have been fulfilled. We must be prepared with treatment, cures, and inoculations. In the meantime know that there is a divine purpose for everything, even AIDS, and that those suffering with it are indeed performing a profound service for all of humankind.

There are many gay men, lesbians, and enlightened heterosexuals whose roles in this AIDS epidemic are to be part of the support team. They are the physicians, researchers, comforters, friends, helpers, financiers, and soft shoulders. We are all in this disease/war together, for good reason, and it is impossible to say which role is the most difficult or the most important.

Let's just always try to remember there is indeed perfection. Even AIDS fits into a perfect scheme, and it can only be for good.

CHAPTER NINETEEN

## *The Call Home*

In the chapter on love I said sex is a major step toward going *home*. Sex helps us to focus on the creative juices of love. The feelings of sex are intense and are found too seldom on earth at this time. They rekindle that love we were so familiar with at home, where we wallowed in the sweet taste of love. It was the common, always present experience, instead of a once-in-a-while treat.

We love sex. We say we are making love because we are. Indeed, it reminds us of who we are and where we came from and refreshes our memory of our Self. There is also another way to refresh our memory. It's the language of God. Let me explain.

As we learned in Chapter Five, everything in creation boils down to love—the unified field in physics. The field of love is the common denominator of everything. It is the basis of everything on earth. It is also the basis of everything back *home*, even if that is thousands of light years away. It wouldn't matter if our home star system is made of elements or metals unimaginable on earth, *home* is still made from the same ingredient: love.

In his Special Relativity, Einstein showed that matter and energy are the same. The rock on Mount Everest is just energy, as air is also just energy. All the metals, the gases, plant and animal cells, and everything else is energy, which is really just another name for vibration. The whole spectrum of all the different energies in creation boils down to infinite combinations of different frequencies and amplitudes of vibration.

Keeping this simple concept in mind, it should be easy to see creation as a wide spectrum of love. Remember, love is another word for Einstein's Unified Field, another word for energy, another word for vibration. At one end of the spectrum of love is the unmanifest silence. Then the slightest vibration appears. It becomes many different combinations of vibration, all varying in frequency and amplitude. The vibrations get more complex and specialized as they endlessly combine with each other. Eventually, they turn into gases. Then they become solid objects, which still are just forms of the vibrating energy.

Even our thoughts are part of this spectrum of vibrating energy. Thought-forms can be pinpointed someplace along the scale as a variation in the infinite variety of vibrations. Some thought-forms are universal Truth and are found throughout creation. Others, here on earth particularly, are error beliefs and are only found where the beliefs are held.

If we had more advanced scientific instruments, we could trace a physical object, like a tree, through the entire spectrum of various levels of energy, clear down to the unmanifest silence. Each lesser vibration would essentially be what we can label *a more refined state* of the tree. At some point in the refined states, we encounter the vibration of sound. This is simply the vibration of the "tree" at the frequency and amplitude that our ears could hear.

Suppose we spoke a language that sounds just like the vibration that it represents? That is, instead of hearing "tree," we would hear what it really sounds like in its more refined state.

The earth's spoken words do not have this connection to the infinite expressions of creation. For instance, in no modern language does the word *Master* vibrate like the cosmic concept of *Master*—and yes, concepts are thought-forms that are also energy. In the case of *Master*, the thought-form is of universal Truth and found throughout creation. If our languages did vibrate like what they represented, our lives would be very, very different, especially if there were no error beliefs. This is the language of God. This is the universal language of the universe. It is the language back *home.*

Using this language of God, we would quickly manifest our true desires. To say or think the cosmic vibration for *Master* would raise our level of awareness to being a Master very quickly. When we tap into the refined state of what we want, and when we speak out its vibration, we enliven the vibrations along the whole spectrum. We would quickly dip into the infinite and manifest in the physical. There are human beings who can put out their hands and manifest gems. They do that with this process of pure thinking along with clear awareness, belief, and intention.

Even in our modern languages we do set into motion these same principles, but to a lesser extent. With a perfect language having the sound of the exact vibration of what we want to manifest, the process would be hastened many-fold.

Although very limited, we on earth do have some words from this language. When we hear these words, our inner feelings for who we are and where we came from are enlivened. Their mere utterance raises our earth vibration to be at one with the vibration back *home*. Then we experience the love we are, a love we long to remember.

I believe the experience is similar to a type of neurolinguistic training where a person is taught to think of a pleasant past experience. That brings the joy or peace associated with it. These words elicit the feelings of past memories, except the memories are pre-birth, from a time/place we innerly associate with *home.*

These cosmic words are no secret. The great meditations of the world—down through the ages in all civilizations and religions—have used these words in their prayers. Often they're called mantras, but the label is immaterial.

As spiritual people we can have our cosmic words to think or speak out. When we do, we'll raise our own vibration to cosmic consciousness. Most importantly, we'll be raising the vibration of planet earth and all humankind here. Packed within these words are tremendous cleansing powers. They cut through and destroy error beliefs of mass-consciousness. They dissolve hate among nations. They bring a truce to the human war against nature. Everything is brought into line with cosmic purpose.

Some of the words we are lucky to have on earth from this language of God are words that describe aspects of *Mastership.* By saying or thinking these words, we quickly bring into our own lives the quality the word represents. That is the *law of quickest manifestation.* We quickly regain our memory of the Master we are, while elevating all our other brothers and sisters at the same time.

There are four basic phrases we'll use, all centering around the various qualities of being a Master. For the correct pronunciation, the words are phonically written in Spanish, including rolling the Rs. An "I" sounds like a long E, as in seed. An "E" sounds like a long A, as in hay. An "A" sounds like the A in father. The more perfect the pronunciation, the better, but even an approximation has powerful vibrations.

In each phrase is the word *Nama.* This means "I bow down with an open heart in reverence." In each of these phrases, you are bowing down to your own Self, the Master you truly are. Here now is our last spirexual experience, *Our Master Selves.*

The first phrase is: *ARIHANTANUM NAMA.* Arihantanum is your pure spirit that knows no obstacles and no limitations.

The second phrase is: *SIDDHANUM NAMA.* Siddhanum is your enlightened soul that is all love and all knowledge, as God created you.

The third phrase is: *UVACHAYIANUM NAMA.* Uvachayianum is the Master in you that teaches love and Truth by example and by just being.

The fourth phrase is: *SAHUNUM NAMA.* Sahunum represents the Saint you are who is simple, above all else.

There is no special way to use these phrases. You can think them, say them aloud, chant them with or without music, or read them. You can do this alone, or in a group.

It would be good to keep in mind the meaning of each phrase, but even that isn't necessary. The vibration of each word carries the message to your inner being.

You can repeat each phrase, one after the other, or you can repeat each phrase many times before going on to the next. You can use all four in any combination, or choose one or two to emphasize.

It's quite simple. How you use *Our Master Selves* is entirely up to you. What you do will no doubt change from time to time. Share these phrases with anyone who might appreciate them, but keep them sacred. They truly are words of the universe and a call home. Wherever you go in the entire creation, these vibrations have the same meaning and intensity.

## OUR MASTER SELVES
*Cosmic Sounds Vibrating Master Qualities*

*Think, say, chant, or read these phrases in any combination. They are spelled phonetically in Spanish.*
Arihantanum Nama
Siddhanum Nama
Uvachayianum Nama
Sahunum Nama

# CHAPTER TWENTY

# *Spirexuality Is*

*Spirexuality* is spirituality,
    Is the connection of sex with spirituality.
*Spirexuality* is the dawning of sexual acceptance,
    Is the dawning of our spirituality,
        Is the dawning of enlightenment.
*Spirexuality* is conscious connection to our Self,
    Is our conscious source for Truth,
        Is our path for practical guidance.
*Spirexuality* is knowing love,
    Is giving our love,
        Is giving our hearts,
            Is receiving love,
                Is receiving hearts.
*Spirexuality* is recognizing the image of God,
    Is being happy,
        Is being joyful,
            Is being blissful,
    Is being light,
        Is being intelligence,
            Is being abundance.
*Spirexuality* is our Creator connection,
    Is being timeless,
        Is being everywhere for all time,
            Is being without judgment,
    Is being perfection,
        Is being infinite energy,
            Is being gentle.

*Spirexuality* is for special friends,
Is growing into oneness with each other,
Is feeling the Unified Field,
Is focusing on love,
Is cuddling.
*Spirexuality* is generating true forgiveness,
Is knowing there is nothing to forgive,
Is for giving and receiving love.
*Spirexuality* is social responsibility,
Is correcting mass-consciousness,
Is group commitment,
Is slashing error beliefs,
Is group channeling.
*Spirexuality* is recognizing divinity in everyone,
Is knowing we're created in God's image,
Is peace and respect for everybody,
Is being without judgment.
*Spirexuality* is our relationship reality,
Is our connection to our relationships,
Is our source for relationships,
Is our answer to challenges.
*Spirexuality* is our connection to our soul,
Is our soul site,
Is peace and well being.
*Spirexuality* is beauty,
Is giving praise to our own beauty,
Is praising everyone's beauty,
Is bellowing out the beauty.
*Spirexuality* is loving our bodies,
Is being grateful to our bodies,
Is bonding with our bodies,
Is filling our body's needs.
*Spirexuality* is public openness,
Is open recognition we are in God's image,
Is open acceptance of our sex,
Is open affection,
Is a public pat.

*Spirexuality* is manifesting our true desires,
  Is discovering our highest goals,
    Is thinking what we are to be,
      Is creating.
*Spirexuality* is channeling our Masters,
  Is receiving answers from our Masters,
    Is receiving Truth from our Masters.
*Spirexuality* is spreading light,
  Is expounding Truth,
    Is radiating love.
*Spirexuality* is knowing who we are,
  Is knowing we have a divine purpose here,
    Is receiving cosmic energies,
      Is perceiving our holy tasks,
        Is accepting our roles.
*Spirexuality* is being grateful for our mission,
  Is unifying again and again and again,
    Is dissipating negativism.
*Spirexuality* is hearing the language of God,
  Is chanting the vibration of the cosmos,
    Is calling home.
*Spirexuality* is being a Master of creation,
  Is being a Master with creation,
    Is being a Master in Creation.

# BOOK ORDER FORM

## unified PUBLICATIONS
1050 University Avenue, Suite 103
San Diego, California 92103

_____copies of GAY SPIRITUALITY
    @ $9.95 each                                                          $_____

Less Discount:
    20% for 2-4 books
    40% for 5-99 books
    50% for 100 or more books               $_____

Subtotal                                      $_____

Within California, add 7% sales tax     $_____

Postage and Handling:
    first book $1.50,
    each additional copy add $.50       $_____

TOTAL AMOUNT ENCLOSED
(USA check or money order)          $_____

NAME_____

ADDRESS_____

CITY _____

STATE AND ZIP _____